NOODLES

OVER 100 RECIPES FOR PERFECT PASTA, REVOLUTIONARY RAMEN, AND PHENOMENAL PHO

Noodles

13-Digit ISBN: 978-1-60433-835-5
10-Digit ISBN: 1-60433-835-0

This book may be ordered by mail from the publisher. Please include $5.99 for postage and handling. Please support your local bookseller first!

Books published by Cider Mill Press Book Publishers are available at special discounts for bulk purchases in the United States by corporations, institutions, and other organizations. For more information, please contact the publisher.

Cider Mill Press Book Publishers
"Where good books are ready for press"
PO Box 454
12 Spring Street
Kennebunkport, Maine 04046
Visit us online! www.cidermillpress.com

Typography: Sentinel, Bushcraft, Helvetica Rounded
Photos by Serena Cosmo appear on pages 30, 33, 35, 36, 42, 47, 65, 69, 75, 76, 79, 89, 91, 97, 98, 105, 109, 113, 117, 127, 132, 135, 138, 144, 187, 191, 194, 200, 205, 221, 230, 233, 235, 239, 240, 243, 253, 259, 261, 262, 264
All other photos are used under official license from Shutterstock.com

Printed in China
1 2 3 4 5 6 7 8 9 0
First Edition

NOODLES

OVER 100 RECIPES FOR PERFECT PASTA, REVOLUTIONARY RAMEN, AND PHENOMENAL PHO

CIDER MILL
PRESS

BOOK
PUBLISHERS
KENNEBUNKPORT, MAINE

Contents

Introduction

Versatile, wholesome, and inexpensive, noodles were destined to become universally beloved. Providing the proverbial blank canvases upon which some of the world's most popular dishes have been crafted, they are the rare item that can withstand any shift in taste and accommodate every culinary trend. Blessing each plate or bowl they grace with feelings of comfort and care, they have transcended their humble composition (flour, eggs, and water) to become the cornerstone of cuisines around the globe.

Despite this considerable tradition, their day is far from over. As the increasingly hectic pace of the world beckons us away from the kitchen, noodles are a tie to the vital and enriching act of taking a step back to provide sustenance for our loved ones and ourselves. There are days when concocting a meal is the last thing one wants to think about, but thanks to noodles' adaptability and ease of preparation, there's always a way past this apprehension.

Since the affection for all things noodle is undeniable, we thought it would be worth fueling the fire. With instructions on how to whip up fresh noodles, Italian standards, Asian classics, comforting soups, indulgent baked offerings, and more, we're certain that even the most zealous noodle enthusiast will find something to warm his or her heart.

Dig in. You'll soon see why we believe that noodles are one of the best testaments to humanity's limitless creativity and ingenuity.

MAKING YOUR OWN NOODLES

Making your own noodles is not rocket science. At the end of the day, it can be as simple as combining two ingredients, eggs and flour, or flour and water. Should you decide to use the all-purpose flour in your food pantry and high-quality eggs, you'll make noodles more delicious than anything you could purchase fresh from the market, even those from high-end grocers. Your noodles will be tender and absolutely satisfying and your journey can end right there.

If, on the other hand, you would like to delve deeper into understanding the subtleties of the ingredients that go into noodle making, read on. Once you begin experimenting with different types of flour and ingredients you will soon be able to discern the slightest of differences, which is a profoundly satisfying development.

Flour: The Foundation of Noodles

A passion for making noodles translates into knowledge of flour. There's no way around it. Otherwise, it is like wanting to master the piano without understanding anything about chord structure. Looking closer at the different flours used to construct your favorite noodles is a great way to enhance your experience, so dive in.

Protein (and Gluten) in Flour: Before we embark on introducing the main types of flour that will aid your noodle-making exploits, it is important to understand the role that protein plays in flour and how it affects the dough. Once water is added to flour and the kneading process begins, two proteins, glutenin and gliadin, come into contact and form a bond that creates a continuous network of fine strands in the dough known as gluten. This network is what gives dough its structure and strength.

In the seminal book *On Food and Cooking*, author and food scientist Harold McGee relates that the Chinese call gluten "the muscle of flour." It is an apt description, as gluten gives dough its elasticity and plasticity, which is the ability to take on a shape and keep it. The right amount of gluten results in a pasta dough that is easier to knead, to roll through the pasta maker, and to stretch without tearing when handled. This explains why bread flour contains higher amounts of protein and why noodles, which need to be more malleable, require less.

Wheat: For thousands of years, the wheat plant crossbred arbitrarily with other plants and grasses, evolving into several different wheat species. One of them, *Triticum aestivum*, proved particularly desirable because it contains glutenin, which produced a more elastic and malleable dough that was easier to shape. We began to cultivate this particular species more than 8,000 years ago, and it now accounts for 90 percent of the wheat grown around the world.

Within the *T. aestivum* genus, wheat is generally categorized by whether it is hard or soft, red or white, winter or spring. For the purposes of this book, we will focus on flours that tend to fall within the soft (less gluten, more malleable dough), red (more flavorful, or "wheatier"), and winter (slightly less gluten than spring) categories, as they tend to produce better tasting noodles that have a slightly chewy yet tender texture.

Accounting for most of the remaining 10 percent of world wheat production is *Triticum durum*, known as durum wheat. Similar to *T. aestivum*, it originated in the Middle East and spread to many parts of the Mediterranean Basin before the spread of the Roman Empire. Deep amber in color and rich in protein, durum wheat is ground into semolina flour and used to make almost all of the dry pasta that is sold commercially. Durum wheat differentiates itself considerably from other grains because its flour contains the gluten protein gliadin, which is extensible rather than elastic. This means that its dough can be rolled easily into sheets so the resulting pasta dries without breaking and reliably holds intricate shapes.

Before we begin exploring the different flours used in noodle making, it is worth noting that flour is not a static product. If "a rose is a rose is a rose" in Gertrude Stein's world, then "flour is not flour is not flour" in ours. In other words, the bag of flour in your pantry is probably very different from your next-door neighbor's. In

fact, flour varies greatly depending on whether it comes from a nearby mill, a regional manufacturer, or a nationally recognized one. That's because when flour is milled, its composition, and thus performance, depends on the wheat grain variety, growing season, the soil in which it is grown, protein content, milling technique, temperature of the grain at the time of milling, and storage. National brands are the exception. Blended specifically for consistency, they combine different hard and soft wheat varieties to guarantee certain protein-level compositions in their flour. Because of this, they are often the flour of choice among professional bakers, who value predictability and consistency above all else.

Ultimately, the decision is yours. As I mentioned earlier, fresh noodles made with a national brand of flour and good, quality eggs will be delicious. Its only shortcoming will be its flavor, which will be rather neutral and contain none of the aromatic notes of nuts, tobacco, and even grass that you would find in a freshly milled flour.

Unbleached All-Purpose Flour: Typically produced from a blend of hard, high-protein bread flours and soft, low-protein pastry flours, all-purpose flour contains a moderate level of protein that ranges from 9 percent to 12 percent in national flour brands, but that can go as low as 7.5 percent in small regional brands. Blended and milled to be versatile, it is strong enough to make bread and soft enough to create tender, delicate scones, cakes, and biscuits. It also makes perfectly tender noodles, though combining it with other flours such as durum wheat or semolina results in tastier and

slightly firmer noodles. Avoid bleached flour whenever possible, as it is treated with chemicals like benzoyl peroxide and chlorine to speed up the flour's aging process. The unbleached version is aged naturally through oxidation. All-purpose flour is also available pre-sifted, a process that aerates the flour to make it lighter than standard all-purpose flour. However, since all flour has a tendency to settle and become more compact during storage, it is advisable to always sift flour before using.

"00" Flour: Produced from soft wheat, finely ground, and almost talcum-like, "00" flour is fairly low in protein content. It is the flour of choice in most Italian homes and among Chinese noodle makers because it produces soft dough that is easy to roll and yields pastas and noodles that are smooth and silky. Tender egg pastas such as tagliatelle, garganelli, and corzetti have most likely been prepared with "00" dough and eggs. Occasionally the categorization of "00" flour causes some confusion because despite always being finely milled, it can be made from soft or hard varieties of wheat and consequently contains different percentages of protein by weight. Soft wheat is lower in protein and creates soft and tender noodles that readily absorb and take on the flavor of a tasty sauce. Hard wheat is higher in gluten content and creates a sturdy dough that is ideal for trapping air bubbles, like bread dough, but that makes it almost impossible to roll out into sheets for pasta. When purchasing it, you will find "00" flour designated for bread and pizza or for pasta, with protein contents ranging from 5 percent to 12 percent. Be sure to select the "00" flour designated for making pasta and not for bread. If this flour is not readily available in your area, it is only a click away on the internet.

Semolina Flour and Durum Flour: Both types of flour come from milling protein-rich durum wheat berries and have the highest protein contents of any flour. Semolina comes from milling the innermost layer, called the endosperm, of the berry. It is characteristically coarse and golden yellow in color as a result of its high concentration of carotenoids (the same compounds responsible for the carrot's orange color). It creates a strong pasta dough that holds any shape and strengthens when heated. Experienced pasta makers often add small amounts of semolina flour to pasta dough made predominantly with "00" flour to add a pleasant chewiness and subtle nutty flavor, and to increase the dough's elasticity during rolling. Semolina flour also makes an excellent alternative to cornmeal, and can be used to dust noodles and noodle-making surfaces. Occasionally, the word semolina causes some confusion because it is also used to describe the innermost layer of any grain, such as corn and rice.

Durum flour has a very fine texture that makes it look like yellow-hued all-purpose flour. A by-product of milling semolina flour, it creates a malleable dough that is easily fed through pasta makers and will curl or bend during cooking.

Again, if these flours are not readily available in your area, look for them online.

Whole Wheat Flour: Ground from hard red spring or winter wheat, this flour consists of the entire wheat berry: endosperm, germ, and bran. Brownish and lightly speckled, whole wheat adds a full-bodied and wheat-y flavor that, due to the tannins in the outer bran, can verge on bitter. Chock-full of naturally occurring vitamins, minerals, and fiber, it is a viable option for health-oriented individuals who don't mind its strong flavor. For better results, it is advisable to add some all-purpose flour to make the resulting dough more pliable and the noodles more tender. Whole wheat flour tends to absorb more moisture than white flour, so you'll need to adjust for that if you're making a substitution in a recipe. There is also white whole wheat flour, which is ground from hard white spring or winter wheat berries; it possesses the same nutritional profile as whole wheat flour but is milder in flavor and lighter in color.

Eggs: Tender Noodles' Not-So-Secret Ingredient

For the purposes of making noodles, or eating the best, most wholesome food possible for that matter, it is best to secure the best-quality eggs available to you.

Eggs play a vital role in many fresh noodle recipes. Not only do they enrich the noodles from a nutritional standpoint, they also add an appealing pale yellow color and a subtle egg flavor to the dough. Eggs also contribute two additional elements that are more important to a noodle maker. First, they provide more protein, which, when combined with the gluten in the dough, enhances the structure of the dough, making it elastic, soft, and easier to roll out thinly without tearing, resulting in tender, smooth, and springy noodles. Secondly, the egg whites give additional

heft and firmness to the dough while preventing the loss of starch as the noodles cook.

It is important to use eggs that have a vibrantly orange yolk, as it is a sign of a healthy, happy, and well-fed chicken. Egg yolks get their color from carotenoids, which are also responsible for strengthening the chicken's immune system. Because chickens only lay eggs if they have sufficient levels of carotenoids, the yolks possess deep hues of dark gold and orange. Paler yolks are often a result of chickens feeding on barley or white cornmeal, foods that don't nourish them as completely as a carotenoid-enhancing diet based on yellow corn and marigold petals.

Using brown or white eggs is up to the discretion of the individual, since they both share the same nutritional profiles and taste the same. Aliza

Green, connoisseur and author of the wonderful book *Making Artisan Pasta*, makes a good argument for buying brown eggs. First, brown eggs come from larger breeds that eat more, take longer to produce their eggs, and produce eggs with thicker protective shells, which prevents internal moisture loss over time, thus helping them maintain their freshness. Also, because brown eggs are considered a specialty product, she adds, their quality tends to be higher.

The quality and freshness of an egg and its temperature at time of use (it's always best to use eggs at room temperature because the flour has an easier time absorbing them) are more important than size or weight.

Eggs in the United States are graded according to the thickness of their shell and the firmness of their egg whites. Agricultural advances have made it possible for large egg producers to assess the quality of each individual egg and to efficiently sort them by size, weight, and quality. With almost scientific precision, eggs are graded AA (top quality), A (good quality, and what is found in most supermarkets), and B (substandard eggs with thin shells and watery egg whites that don't reach consumers but are used commercially and industrially). They are also further categorized by size: medium, large (the most common size), and extra large. The past decade or so has also seen a rise in popularity of free-range and organic eggs. The product of smaller-scale enterprises, these chickens are fed organic feed and are caged with slightly more space at their disposal than standard chicken farms. While the jury is still out on whether this last category tastes better, it nonetheless constitutes an additional, and perhaps politically oriented, option for noodle makers.

For the purposes of making noodles, it is best to secure the freshest eggs available, so check the expiration dates before buying them and buy them when they are well within that window.

In making noodles it is important to avoid cold, so use room temperature eggs. Also, do not work on a naturally cold surface such as marble or stainless steel. Wood is best; otherwise Corian or linoleum will work. If you do not make perfect dough the first time, don't be discouraged.

Water

The water you use can influence dough quality depending on its mineral content and temperature.

Mineral-rich water from your tap is best for making noodles. The only exception is if your water is particularly hard, or excessively high in minerals like magnesium and calcium. In that case, you may be better off using spring water, as too much of these minerals can produce a tighter gluten network in the dough and result in a firmer, and sometimes too firm, dough.

Always use tepid water, around 105°F (or two parts cold water to one part boiling water), as it makes it easier for the flour to absorb the liquid. Exceptions to this guideline exist and generally involve Asian noodles that require boiling water to activate gluten.

Salt

Using a pinch or two of fine-grain iodized salt (table salt) or slightly coarser kosher salt both work nicely and contribute a hint of salty flavor to your noodles. Try to avoid using fine or coarse sea salt, as their high mineral content can cause dough to develop a tighter gluten network, resulting in a firmer, and sometimes too firm, noodle.

Pasta Doughs & Fresh Noodles

The dream of making fresh pasta is a common one. It is a fantasy that is also frequently drowned out by the ease of opening a box and dumping its contents into a pot of boiling water. Too often, in our opinion. Because there's nothing out of reach about whipping up a simple dough, letting it rest, and running it through a pasta maker before cutting it into your desired shape (since you're enough of a noodle-phile to page through a book built entirely around them, we're assuming that you already have a pasta maker. But if not, better-than-satisfactory versions are available for around $30 or $40).

Making your own noodles isn't miraculous; it only tastes like it. This chapter intends to introduce you to a few basic doughs that will help you turn out classic noodles like spaghetti, linguine, and Chinese egg noodles, as well as a few off-the-beaten path options that will soon become as cherished as those standards. So start fresh, and shift pasta from a last-resort dish to an immersive experience that everyone looks forward to.

USING YOUR PASTA MAKER

1 Once you have cut and rolled your dough, set the pasta maker for the flat roller (no teeth) on the widest setting (typically notch 1). Now feed the dough into the rollers. As a rather rough, thick sheet comes out the other end, make sure to support it with your hand or fingers. Fold the sheet of dough over itself twice, as you would a letter, and then turn the folded dough on its side and feed it back into the machine again. Repeat this folding and feeding back into the machine three more times. This process is called "laminating" and it makes the dough more sturdy and easier to handle.

2 Set the machine to the second-widest setting (typically notch 2) and feed the dough into the rollers. Again, support the pasta as it comes out the other side. Again, fold it as you would a letter and feed it into the rollers on its short side; repeat this three more times.

3 Set the machine to the third-widest setting (typically notch 3) and feed the dough into the rollers. Again, support the pasta as it comes out the other side. Again, fold it as you would a letter and feed it into the rollers on its short side; repeat this three more times.

4 Set the machine to the second-smallest setting (typically notch 4). Feed the pasta into the rollers. Again, support the pasta as it comes out the other side. At this point, there is no need to laminate the pasta.

Stop rolling at this point if making sheets of pasta for maltagliati, farfalle, and cappellacci. If you like your fettuccine, pappardelle, and tagliatelle a little thicker, then this is the setting for you.

5 Set the machine to the smallest setting (typically notch 5). Cut the pasta sheet in half and feed it into the rollers. Again, support the pasta as it comes out the other side.

This last setting makes pasta sheets about $1/16$ inch thick, which is so thin that you can see through them. If you like your fettuccine, pappardelle, and tagliatelle very thin, then this is the setting for you.

The just rolled pasta will be very delicate, so be gentle handling it. If the pasta sheet is too long to easily handle, carefully cut it in half. Lightly dust each sheet with flour and lay it on a surface lined with wax or parchment paper. Repeat all of the above steps with the remaining pieces of dough.

6 The dough needs to be allowed to dry for approximately 15 minutes after

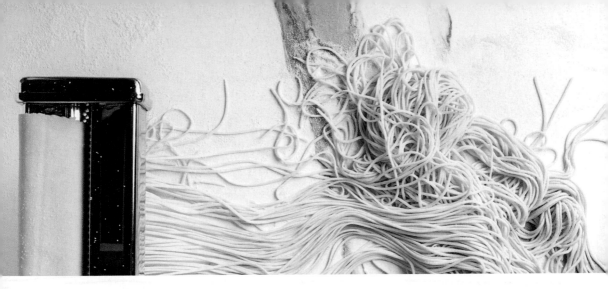

it has been rolled out and before it is cut into strands or other shapes. This drying time makes the dough less sticky and easier to handle. Keep in mind that when the pasta is very thick or wide it will need to be turned over to ensure thorough and even drying (not necessary for thin noodles). Pasta sheets are now ready to be shaped or cut according to recipe requirements. The notable exception to this rule is if you are making stuffed pasta. In this case, not letting the dough dry is best because the slight stickiness helps the pasta adhere better and creates a better seal.

7 Once fresh pasta has been cut, toss it with semolina flour, place it on a lightly floured surface (again, with semolina flour), and allow it to dry for at least 15 minutes before cooking. This drying period is important because it allows the pasta to become firmer and less sticky, which prevents the pasta from sticking together as it cooks (noodles also hold their shape better when allowed to dry slightly before cooking). More specific drying times are indicated in individual recipes. Just note that the drying process can be fickle. Depending on temperature, humidity levels, and the size of the noodles, the process may take a longer or shorter period of time than stated in the recipes. It is probably best to avoid making noodles on very humid days. If you can't avoid it, turn on the air conditioning or even a movable fan to help the air circulate more effectively.

Three-Egg Basic Pasta Dough

YIELD: ABOUT 1 POUND • ACTIVE TIME: 1 HOUR
TOTAL TIME: 2 TO 3 HOURS

This recipe is your standard, go-to recipe when you want to simplify the pasta-making process and still get delicious dough.

INGREDIENTS

2¾ cups all-purpose flour, plus more for dusting

3 large eggs

1 egg yolk

2 tablespoons tepid water, plus more as needed

1 On a flat work surface, form the flour into a mound. Create a well in the center, then add the eggs, egg yolk, and the 2 tablespoons of water. Using a fork or your fingertips, gradually start pulling the flour into the pool of egg, beginning with the flour at the inner rim of the well. Continue to gradually add flour until the dough starts holding together in a single floury mass, adding more water—1 tablespoon at a time—if the mixture is too dry to stick together. Once the dough feels firm and dry, and can form a craggy-looking ball, it's time to start kneading.

2 Begin by working the remaining flour on the work surface into the ball of dough. Using the heel of your hand, push the ball of dough away from you in a downward motion. Turn the dough 45 degrees each time you repeat this motion, as doing so incorporates the flour more evenly. As you continue to knead, you'll notice the dough getting less and less floury. Eventually, it will have a smooth, elastic texture. If the dough still feels wet, tacky, or sticky, dust it with flour and continue kneading. If it feels too dry and is not completely sticking together, wet your hands with water and continue kneading. Wet your hands as many times as you need in order to help the dough shape into a ball. Knead for 8 to 10 minutes. It seems like a long time, but it creates a dough that is smooth and springy, and eliminates any air bubbles and bits of unincorporated flour in the dough. The dough has been sufficiently kneaded when it is very smooth and gently pulls back into place when stretched.

3 Wrap the ball of dough tightly in clear food wrap and let rest for 1 hour, but 2 hours is even better if you have the time. If using within a few hours, leave it out on the kitchen counter, otherwise refrigerate it (it will keep for up to 3 days). If you do refrigerate it, however, the dough may experience some discoloration (but it won't affect the flavor at all).

4 Cut the dough into four even pieces. Set one piece on a smooth work surface and wrap up the rest in clear food wrap to prevent drying. Shape the dough into a ball, place it on the surface, and, with the palm of your hand, push down on it so that it looks like a thick pita. Using a rolling pin, roll the dough to ½-inch thick. Try as much as possible to keep the thickness and width of the dough "patty" even, as it will help the dough fit through the pasta maker more easily. When you're ready to run it through the pasta maker, turn to page 20.

TIP: THIS DOUGH IS SUITABLE FOR POPULAR NOODLES SUCH AS FETTUCCINE, PAPPARDELLE, TAGLIATELLE, AND FARFALLE.

All Yolk Pasta Dough

YIELD: ¾ POUND · ACTIVE TIME: 1 HOUR
TOTAL TIME: 2 TO 3 HOURS

Dough made exclusively with egg yolks has a beautiful rich and golden color, and makes smooth and very tender pasta. It is an excellent dough for making thin, fragile pasta strands or miniature filled pasta.

INGREDIENTS

1½ cups all-purpose flour

⅓ cup finely milled "00" flour, plus more as needed

8 large egg yolks

2 tablespoons tepid water, plus more as needed

1 On a flat work surface, form the flour into a mound. Create a well in the center, then add the egg yolks and the 2 tablespoons of water. Using a fork or your fingertips, gradually start pulling the flour into the pool of egg, beginning with the flour at the inner rim of the well. Continue to gradually add flour until the dough starts holding together in a single floury mass, adding more water—1 tablespoon at a time—if the mixture is too dry to stick together. Once the dough feels firm and dry, and can form a craggy-looking ball, it's time to start kneading.

2 Begin by working the remaining flour on the work surface into the ball of dough. Using the heel of your hand, push the ball of dough away from you in a downward motion. Turn the dough 45 degrees each time you repeat this motion, as doing so incorporates the flour more evenly. As you continue to knead, you'll notice the dough getting less and less floury. Eventually it will have a smooth, elastic texture. If the dough still feels wet, tacky, or sticky, dust it with flour and continue kneading. If it feels too dry and is not completely sticking together, wet your hands with water and continue kneading. Wet your hands as many times as you need in order to help the dough shape into a ball. Knead for 8 to 10 minutes. It seems like a long time, but it creates a dough that is smooth and springy, and eliminates any air bubbles and bits of unincorporated flour in the dough. The dough has been sufficiently kneaded when it is very smooth and gently pulls back into place when stretched.

3 Wrap the ball of dough tightly in clear food wrap and let rest for 1 hour, but 2 hours is even better if you have the time. If using within a few hours, leave it out on the kitchen counter, otherwise refrigerate it (it will keep for up to 3 days). If you do refrigerate it, however, the dough may experience some discoloration (but it won't affect the flavor at all).

4 Cut the dough into four even pieces. Set one piece on a smooth work surface and wrap up the rest in clear plastic wrap to prevent drying. Shape the dough into a ball, place it on the surface, and, with the palm of your hand, push down on it so that it looks like a thick pita. Using a rolling pin, roll the dough to $\frac{1}{2}$-inch thick. Try as much as possible to keep the thickness and width of the dough "patty" even, as it will help the dough fit through the pasta maker more easily. When you're ready to run it through the pasta maker, turn to page 20.

TIP: THIS DOUGH IS SUITABLE FOR POPULAR NOODLES SUCH AS LINGUINE AND SPAGHETTI.

Whole Wheat Pasta Dough

YIELD: 1¾ POUNDS • ACTIVE TIME: 1 HOUR
TOTAL TIME: 2 TO 3 HOURS

This dough is perfect for those devotees of chewy pappardelle or linguine. Whole wheat pasta is also great with thick, creamy sauces.

1 On a flat work surface combine the flour and salt and form it into a mountainlike mound. Create a well in the center, then add the egg yolks, olive oil, and the 2 tablespoons of water. Using a fork or your fingertips, gradually start pulling the flour into the pool of egg, beginning with the flour at the inner rim of the well. Continue to gradually add flour until the dough starts holding together in a single floury mass, adding more water—1 tablespoon at a time—if the mixture is too dry to stick together. Once the dough feels firm and dry, and can form a craggy-looking ball, it's time to start kneading.

2 Begin by working the remaining flour on the work surface into the ball of dough. Using the heel of your hand, push the ball of dough away from you in a downward motion. Turn the dough 45 degrees each time you repeat this motion, as doing so incorporates the flour more evenly. As you continue to knead, you'll notice the dough getting less and less floury. Eventually it will have a smooth, elastic texture. If the dough still feels wet, tacky, or sticky, dust it with flour and continue kneading. If it feels too dry and is not completely sticking together, wet your hands with water and continue kneading. Wet your hands as many times as you need in order to help the dough shape into a ball. Knead for 8 to 10 minutes. It seems like a long time, but it creates a dough that is smooth and springy, and eliminates any air bubbles and bits of unincorporated flour in the dough. The dough has been sufficiently kneaded when it is very smooth and gently pulls back into place when stretched.

INGREDIENTS

**4 cups finely ground whole wheat flour,
plus more as needed**

1½ teaspoons salt

4 large egg yolks

**1 tablespoon
extra virgin olive oil**

**2 tablespoons water,
plus more as needed**

3 Wrap the ball of dough tightly in clear food wrap and let rest for 1 hour, but 2 hours is even better if you have the time. If using within a few hours, leave it out on the kitchen counter, otherwise refrigerate it (it will keep for up to 3 days). If you do refrigerate it, however, the dough may experience some discoloration (but it won't affect the flavor at all).

4 Cut the dough into four even pieces. Set one piece on a smooth work surface and wrap up the rest in clear food wrap to prevent drying. Shape the dough into a ball, place it on the surface, and, with the palm of your hand, push down on it so that it looks like a thick pita. Using a rolling pin, roll the dough to ½-inch thick. Try as much as possible to keep the thickness and width of the dough "patty" even, as it will help the dough fit through the pasta maker more easily. When you're ready to run it through the pasta maker, turn to page 20.

Pizzoccheri

YIELD: 1 POUND • ACTIVE TIME: 1 HOUR
TOTAL TIME: ABOUT 1 HOUR AND 45 MINUTES

This thick, purple-gray noodle hails from northwestern Italy's Valtellina area—though the residents of the canton of Graubünden in Switzerland may dispute this claim. Tasty, chewy, and hearty, it is ideal for harsh winter days.

INGREDIENTS

1 cup buckwheat flour

1 cup all-purpose flour, plus more as needed

½ teaspoon salt, plus more for the pasta water

¼ cup very warm but not boiling water, plus more as needed

2 large eggs

Semolina flour, for dusting

1 Combine all of the ingredients and prepare the dough as directed in Steps 1 and 2 on page 22, letting it rest for 40 minutes. Cut the dough into quarters. Cover three pieces with clear food wrap to prevent them from drying.

2 Rolling the dough using a pasta maker: Lightly flour a piece of dough and, using a rolling pin, roll it into a band about 4 inches wide and 8 inches long. Run the band three times through the widest setting of the pasta maker. The dough will now be 12 to 15 inches long and 4 to 5 inches wide. Repeat this process with the remaining pieces of dough.

Rolling the dough by hand: Using a lightly floured rolling pin, roll a piece of dough into an approximately 10-inch square that is ³⁄₁₆-inch thick, flouring it as little as possible but as much as necessary to keep the dough from sticking to the counter. Repeat this process with the remaining pieces of dough.

3 Regardless of the method in which the pasta has been rolled, hang the dough across a wooden drying rack (a broom handle set up between two chairs works nicely) and air-dry for 30 minutes, turning the sheets over twice during that time.

4 To make the pizzoccheri, lightly flour the surface of a dough sheet and gently roll it up, starting from a short end. Using a very sharp knife, gently slice the roll across into $\frac{1}{3}$-inch-wide ribbons, taking care not to compress the roll too much as you slice through it. Repeat with the remaining pasta sheets. Lightly dust the pasta coils with semolina flour, then unroll them and set on lightly floured parchment paper-lined baking sheets. Air-dry them for 30 minutes, then cook in a large pot of boiling, salted water for 4 to 5 minutes.

Tajarin

YIELD: ½ POUND • ACTIVE TIME: 2½ HOURS
TOTAL TIME: 3½ HOURS

Rich and golden, these very thin, flat noodles most often appear alongside roasted meats such as veal, pork, and chicken.

1 Prepare the dough as directed, rolling the dough to the thinnest setting (generally notch 5) for pasta sheets that are about ¹⁄₁₆-inch thick. Cut into 8-inch-long sheets. Lay the pasta sheets on lightly floured parchment paper-lined baking sheets. Air-dry for 15 minutes.

2 Working with one pasta sheet at a time, lightly dust it with semolina flour, then gently roll it up, starting from a short end. Using a very sharp knife, gently slice the roll across into ¹⁄₁₂-inch-wide strips. Lightly dust the cut roll with flour, then gently begin unfolding the strips, one by one, as you shake off any excess flour. Arrange them either straight and spread out or curl them in a coil. Repeat with all the pasta sheets. Allow them to air-dry for 30 minutes and then cook. Alternatively, you can place them, once air-dried, on a baking sheet, cover with a kitchen towel, and refrigerate for up to 3 days.

3 To cook the tajarin, bring a large pot of salted water to boil. Cook until the pasta is tender but still chewy, typically for no more than 2 minutes. Drain and serve with the sauce of your choice.

INGREDIENTS

All Yolk Pasta Dough (see pages 24–25)

Semolina flour, for dusting

Salt, to taste

Farfalle

**YIELD: ¾ POUND • ACTIVE TIME: 45 MINUTES
TOTAL TIME: 3 HOURS**

These beautiful, butterfly-shaped creations (farfalle means butterfly in Italian) are exceptionally versatile, though they shine brightest when combined with tomato- or cream-based sauces.

INGREDIENTS

All-Yolk Pasta Dough
(see pages 24–25)

Semolina flour,
for dusting

Salt, to taste

1 Prepare the dough as directed, rolling the dough to the second thinnest setting (generally notch 4) for pasta sheets that are about ⅛-inch thick. Lay the pasta sheets on lightly floured parchment paper-lined baking sheets and cover loosely with clear food wrap. Work quickly to keep the pasta sheets from drying out, which makes it harder for the pasta to stick together.

2 Working with one pasta sheet at a time, place it on a lightly floured work surface and trim both ends to create a rectangle. Using a pastry cutter, cut the pasta sheet lengthwise into 1- to 1¼-inch-wide ribbons. Carefully separate the ribbons from each other, then, using a ridged pastry cutter, cut the ribbons into 2-inch pieces. To form the butterfly shape, place the index finger of your nondominant hand on the center of the piece of pasta. Then place the thumb and index finger of your dominant hand on the sides of the rectangle—right in the middle—and pinch the dough together to create a butterfly shape. Firmly pinch the center again to help it hold its shape. Leave the ruffled ends of the farfalle untouched. Repeat with all the pasta sheets. Set the farfalle on lightly floured parchment paper-lined baking sheets so they are not touching. Allow them to air-dry for at least 30 minutes and up to 3 hours, and then cook. Alternatively, you can place them, once air-dried, in a bowl, cover with a kitchen towel, and refrigerate for up to 3 days. Or freeze on the baking sheets, transfer to freezer bags, and store in the freezer for up to 2 months. Do not thaw them prior to cooking (they will become mushy), and add an extra minute or 2 to their cooking time.

3 To cook the farfalle, bring a large pot of salted water to boil. Add the farfalle and cook until the pasta is tender but still chewy, 2 to 3 minutes. Drain and serve with the sauce of your choice.

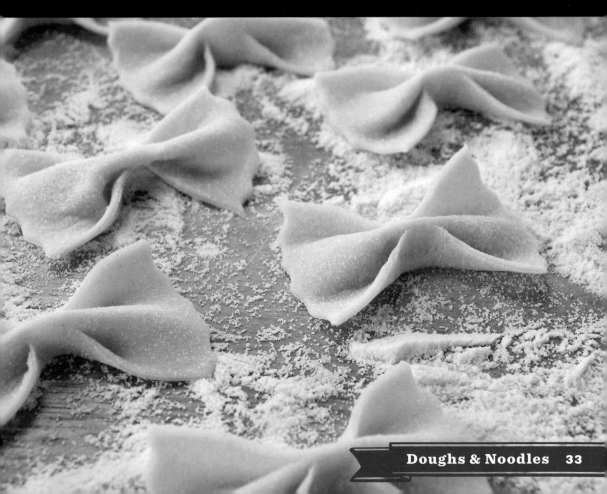

Orecchiette

**YIELD: ABOUT 1 POUND • ACTIVE TIME: 1½ HOURS
TOTAL TIME: 4 TO 5 HOURS**

True to their name ("little ears"), these ear-shaped morsels provide an enjoyable contrast in textures once cooked—the center is thin and soft, while the slightly thicker outer edge is pleasantly chewy.

INGREDIENTS

2 cups semolina flour, plus more for dusting

1 teaspoon salt, plus more for the pasta water

¾ cup water, plus more as needed

1 Combine the flour and salt in a large bowl. Add the water a little at a time while mixing with a fork. Continue mixing the dough until it starts holding together in a single floury mass. If it's still too dry to stick together, add more water, 1 teaspoon at a time, until it does. Work the dough with your hands until it feels firm and dry, and can be formed into a craggy-looking ball.

2 Transfer the dough to a lightly floured work surface and knead it for 10 minutes. Because it is made with semolina flour, the dough can be quite stiff and hard. (You can also mix and knead this in a standing mixer; don't try it with a hand-held mixer—the dough is too stiff and could burn the motor out.) Using the heel of your hand, push the ball of dough away from you in a downward motion. Turn the dough 45 degrees each time you repeat this motion, as doing so incorporates the flour more evenly. Wet your hands as needed if the dough is too sticky. After 10 minutes of kneading, the dough will only be slightly softer (most of the softening is going to occur when the dough rests, which is when the gluten network

within the dough will relax). Shape into a ball, cover tightly with clear food wrap, and let rest in the refrigerator for at least 2 hours and up to 2 days.

3 Cut the dough into four equal sections. Take one dough section and shape it into an oval with your hands. Cover the remaining sections with clear food wrap to prevent it from drying out. Place on a lightly floured work surface and, with the palms of your hands, roll it against the surface until it becomes a long ½-inch-thick rope. Using a sharp paring knife, cut the rope into ¼-inch discs, lightly dusting with semolina flour them so they don't stick together.

4 To form the orecchiette, place a disc on the work surface. Stick your thumb in flour, place it on top of the disc, and, applying a little pressure, drag your thumb, and the accompanying dough, across to create an ear-like shape. Flour your thumb before making each orecchiette for best results. Lightly dust the orecchiette with flour and set them on lightly floured parchment paper-covered baking sheets so they are not touching. Allow them to air-dry for 1 hour, turning them over once halfway through, and then cook. Alternatively, you can place them, once air-dried, in a bowl, cover with a kitchen towel, and refrigerate for up to 3 days.

5 To cook the orecchiette, bring a large pot of salted water to boil. Add the orecchiette and cook until they are tender but still chewy, 3 to 4 minutes. Drain and serve with the sauce of your choice.

Nodi

Inspired by the shape of the gondola, nodi is created by making a knot in a thin rope of dough.

INGREDIENTS

1¾ cups semolina flour, plus more for dusting

1 teaspoon salt, plus more for the pasta water

½ teaspoon fennel seeds, finely ground

⅔ cup warm water

1 Put the flour, salt, and ground fennel in a large bowl and add the water. Begin mixing with a fork until the mixture starts to roughly stick together and look coarse. Gather it together with your hands and transfer it to a lightly floured work surface.

2 Using the heel of your hand, push the ball of dough away from you in a downward motion. Turn the dough 45 degrees each time you repeat this motion, as doing so incorporates the flour more evenly. If the dough feels too dry, wet your hands as many times as you need in order to help shape the dough into a ball. Knead for 10 minutes.

3 Cover the dough tightly with clear food wrap to keep it from drying out and let rest for 1 hour, but 2 hours is even better. If using within a few hours, leave out on the kitchen counter. Otherwise, put it in the refrigerator, where it will keep for up to 3 days.

4 Between the palms of your hands or on a lightly floured work surface, roll the dough into a 2-inch-thick salami and cut it across into 18 rounds of even thickness (the easiest way to do this is to cut the roll in half and continue cutting each piece in half until you have 18 pieces). Cover all the pieces but one to keep them from drying out.

5 With the palms of your hands, roll the piece of dough left out into a long rope $1/8$-inch thick. Now make the knots. Starting on one end of the rope, tie a simple knot, gently pull on both ends to slightly tighten the knot, then cut the knot off the rope, leaving a tail on each side of about $3/8$-inch long. Keep making and cutting off knots in this manner until you use up all of the rope. Repeat with the remaining pieces of dough. Set the finished knots on lightly floured parchment paper-lined baking sheets so they are not touching. Allow them to air-dry for 2 hours, turning them over once halfway through, and then cook. Alternatively, you can place them, once air-dried, in a bowl, cover with a kitchen towel, and refrigerate for up to 3 days.

6 To cook the nodi, place in a large pot of boiling salted water for 2 to 3 minutes, until they are tender but still firm.

Fazzoletti

Square or rectangular in shape, like the thin handkerchiefs they are named for, fazzoletti are easy to make. You don't have to be all that precise in how you cut them; they'll still taste delicious!

INGREDIENTS

Three-Egg Basic Pasta Dough (pages 22–23)

Semolina flour, for dusting

Salt, to taste

1 Prepare the dough as directed, rolling the dough to the thinnest setting (generally notch 5) for pasta sheets that are about $\frac{1}{16}$-inch thick. Lay the pasta sheets on lightly floured parchment paper-lined baking sheets and let them air-dry for 15 minutes.

2 Cut each pasta sheet into as many $2\frac{1}{2}$-inch squares or $1\frac{1}{2}$ x $2\frac{1}{2}$-inch rectangles as possible. Set them on lightly floured parchment paper-covered baking sheets so they are not touching. Gather any scraps together into a ball, put it through the pasta maker to create additional pasta sheets, and cut those as well. Allow them to air-dry for 1 hour, turning them over once halfway, and then cook. Alternatively, you can place them, once air-dried, in a bowl, cover with a kitchen towel, and refrigerate for up to 3 days.

3 To cook the fazzoletti, cook for about 1 minute in a pot of boiling, salted water, until they are tender but still chewy.

Trofie

YIELD: ABOUT 1 POUND • ACTIVE TIME: 40 MINUTES
TOTAL TIME: 3 HOURS

These very thin, chewy spirals are fairly neutral in flavor and are consequently at their best when paired with strongly flavored sauces like pesto and meat ragùs.

1 Put the flour and salt in a large bowl, mix well with a fork, and add the water. Mix with the fork until all the water has been absorbed, then start working the dough with your hands. In a few minutes the crumbly mixture will begin to come together as a grainy dough.

2 Transfer the dough, along with any bits stuck to the bowl, to a lightly floured work surface. Begin to knead the dough. Using the heel of your hand, push the ball of dough away from you in a downward motion. Turn the dough 45 degrees each time you repeat this motion, as doing so incorporates the flour more evenly. Knead the dough for about 10 minutes. Cover the dough with clear food wrap to keep it from drying out and let rest at room temperature for 1 hour, but 2 hours is even better.

3 Between the palms of your hands or on a lightly floured work surface, roll the dough into a 2-inch-thick salami and cut it across into eight pieces (the easiest way to do this is to cut the roll in half and continue cutting each piece in half until you have eight pieces). Cover all the dough pieces but one to keep them from drying out. Shape the piece of dough into a ball, and then roll it until it's a long, ½-inch-thick rope. Cut into ½-inch pieces and dust them with flour.

INGREDIENTS

2¾ cups all-purpose flour

**1 teaspoon salt,
plus more to taste**

1 cup water

Semolina flour, for dusting

4 Working with one piece at a time, press down on the dough with your fingertips and roll the dough down the palm of your other hand. This action will cause the piece of dough to turn into a narrow spiral with tapered ends. Repeat with the remaining pieces of dough. Dust the spirals with flour, set them on flour-dusted, parchment-lined baking sheets, and allow them to air-dry for 2 hours, turning them over halfway through.

5 To cook the trofie, cook for 3 to 4 minutes in a pot of boiling, salted water, until they are tender but still chewy.

INGREDIENTS

2¼ cups semolina flour, plus more for dusting

1½ teaspoons salt, plus more for the pasta water

3 large eggs

2 tablespoons extra virgin olive oil

2 tablespoons water

Garganelli

YIELD: 1½ POUNDS • ACTIVE TIME: 1½ HOURS
TOTAL TIME: 3½ HOURS

Garganelli, yet another of Bologna's many gastronomic contributions, are made by rolling pasta squares into tubes. The dough needs to be pliable and velvety soft in order to be rolled properly, which is best done around a chopstick.

1 Combine all of the ingredients and prepare the dough as directed on pages 22 and 23, and then use a pasta maker to roll the dough to the second-thinnest setting (generally notch 4) for pasta sheets that are about ⅛-inch thick. Lay the pasta sheets on flour-dusted, parchment-lined baking sheets, and cover them loosely with plastic wrap.

2 Working with one pasta sheet at a time, lightly dust it with flour. Cut it into 1½-inch-wide strips and then cut the strips into 1½-inch squares. Repeat with the remaining pasta sheets. Cover the squares loosely with plastic wrap. Gather any scraps together into a ball, put it through the pasta maker to create additional pasta sheets, and cut those as well.

3 To make each garganello, place one square of pasta dough on a lightly floured work surface with one of the corners pointing toward you. Using a chopstick, gently roll the square of pasta around the chopstick, starting from the corner closest to you until a tube forms. Once completely rolled, press down slightly as you seal the ends together, then carefully slide the pasta tube off the chopstick and lightly dust with flour. Set them on flour-dusted, parchment-lined baking sheets and allow them to air-dry for 1 hour, turning them over halfway through.

4 To cook the garganelli, cook for 2 to 3 minutes in a pot of boiling, salted water, until they are tender but still chewy.

Chinese Egg Noodles

This springy, chewy noodle is especially versatile and can be used in lo mein and chow mein dishes as well as soups. It is very forgiving and is an especially excellent option for the novice noodlemaker.

1 Mix the flour and salt together in a large bowl. Add the eggs and mix until a floury dough forms. Add the 3 tablespoons of water and continue to mix until you almost can't see any remaining traces of flour. If you find, even after adding the water, that your dough is still very floury, add more water, 1 tablespoon at a time, and continue mixing it with your hands until the dough starts coming together more easily. Start kneading the dough in the bowl with your dominant hand. Continue kneading in the bowl until a smooth ball forms; this may take about 10 minutes. Wrap the dough tightly in clear plastic wrap, and let rest at room temperature for 40 to 50 minutes to allow the gluten in the dough to relax.

2 Unwrap the dough and place it on a lightly floured work surface. Using a rolling pin, begin "beating" the dough, turning it over after every 10 whacks or so. Continue doing this for 6 minutes. Then shape the dough into a ball, cover with clear food wrap, and let rest at room temperature for another 30 minutes.

3 Return the dough to the work surface (no need to flour again). Cut it in half and wrap one half in clear food wrap to prevent drying. Roll the other half into a large, thin sheet about twice the length and breadth of the length of your rolling pin (you should be able to almost see your hand through it). Lightly flour both sides of the sheet of dough and then fold the sheet of dough twice over itself to create a three-layered fold (like a letter).

4 Using a very sharp knife, slice across the roll into evenly spaced strands. You can make them as thin or thick as you'd like. As you cut the dough, be sure to hold the knife perpendicular to the surface and lightly push the newly cut strip away from the roll with the knife to completely separate it. Continue until you have cut the entire roll, then lightly dust the slivered noodles with flour to prevent any sticking. Transfer the noodles to a parchment-lined baking sheet, shaking off any excess flour if necessary. You can leave them nested or unspool them according to your preference, as either way they will unravel and straighten once boiled. Repeat with the remaining dough. Cook in a pot of boiling, salted water for 3 to 4 minutes, or cover and refrigerate for up to day.

INGREDIENTS

2 cups all-purpose flour, plus more for dusting

1 teaspoon salt, plus more for the pasta water

2 large eggs, lightly beaten

3 tablespoons water, plus more as needed

Udon Noodles

YIELD: 1 POUND • ACTIVE TIME: 1 HOUR
TOTAL TIME: 3 HOURS

Thick, chewy, soft, slippery, and almost irresistibly gummy, Japanese udon noodles are at their best when made fresh, as the packaged dried versions are too thin and short to hold up to hearty flavors.

Stir the water and salt together in a small bowl until the salt dissolves. Put the flour in a large bowl and make a well in the center. Add the salted water in a stream while stirring the flour. Once all the water has been added, begin working the dough with your hands to incorporate all the flour. If the dough is too dry, add water in 1-teaspoon increments until the dough sticks together.

Transfer the dough to a very lightly dusted work surface. Knead the dough with the palm of your dominant hand, turning it 45 degrees with each pressing, until the dough becomes uniformly smooth and it slowly springs back when pressed by a finger, about 10 minutes. Cover the dough tightly with plastic wrap and let rest for 1 to 2 hours to relax the gluten.

Cut the dough into two pieces. Set one on a lightly dusted work surface and wrap the other in plastic wrap to prevent drying. Pat the piece of dough into a rectangular shape and, using a lightly floured rolling pin, roll the dough into a ⅛-inch thick rectangle. Lightly dust the dough and then fold it twice over itself to create a three-layered fold, as you would a letter.

Using a very sharp knife, slice the roll into ⅛-inch-wide strands. As you cut the dough, be sure to hold the knife perpendicular to the surface and lightly push the newly cut strip away from the roll with the knife to completely separate it. Continue until you have cut the entire roll, then lightly dust the slivered pasta to prevent any sticking. Transfer the noodles to a parchment-lined baking sheet, shaking off any excess starch if necessary. Repeat with the remaining dough. Udon noodles quickly turn brittle and break when handled, so cook as soon as you finish making them.

6 To cook the udon, cook for about 1 minute in a pot of boiling, salted water, until they are tender but still chewy.

INGREDIENTS

¼ cup warm water, plus more as needed

1 teaspoon fine sea salt

2¼ cups cake flour or finely milled "00" flour

Potato starch or cornstarch, for dusting

Sauces

Yes, the classic tomato sauce is tough to beat, but sticking to just that is failing to get the most out of your noodles. A large part of them becoming a global sensation is the innumerable flavors they can accommodate, as you'll see from the tempting array presented in this chapter.

The sauces here are only a smattering of what's available out there, but we're betting they keep your beloved noodles from growing stale, and present the hard-to-please, picky eaters in your life something new in an easy-to-accept package.

Tomato Concasse: A number of recipes call for you to remove the skin and seeds from a tomato, as they can be bitter. To do this easily, boil enough water for a tomato to be submerged and add a pinch of salt. Prepare an ice bath and score the top of the tomato with a paring knife. Place the tomato in the boiling water for 30 seconds, carefully remove it, and place it in the ice bath. Once the tomato is cool, remove from ice bath and peel with the paring knife. Cut into quarters and remove the seeds.

Classic Fresh Tomato Sauce

**YIELD: 4 SERVINGS • ACTIVE TIME: 20 MINUTES
TOTAL TIME: 45 MINUTES**

If you're going to the trouble of making sauce from fresh tomatoes, you probably don't want your freezer involved. This recipe deals with such a small quantity of fresh tomatoes that it's quick, easy, and only makes enough for a meal or two.

1 Place the tomatoes in a food processor or blender and puree them.

2 Heat a large skillet large over low heat for 2 to 3 minutes. Add the olive oil (or unsalted butter), raise the heat to medium, and heat for 1 or 2 minutes. Add the onion and a pinch of salt and cook, stirring frequently, until softened, about 10 minutes. Add the tomatoes and two pinches of salt and stir. Bring to a boil, reduce the heat to low, cover, and simmer until thickened, about 20 minutes.

3 Once the sauce is done, place the whole basil leaves, if using, on the surface and close the lid for 5 minutes. The basil will gently perfume the sauce.

INGREDIENTS

4 pounds very ripe plum tomatoes, concasse and chopped

2 tablespoons extra virgin olive oil or unsalted butter

1 medium onion, grated or thinly sliced

Salt, to taste

Handful of basil leaves (optional)

Parmesan cheese, grated

Roasted Tomato and Garlic Sauce

YIELD: 4 SERVINGS • ACTIVE TIME: 15 MINUTES
TOTAL TIME: 2 HOURS

Garlic can be a bit overpowering in most simple tomato sauce recipes; however, the earthy sweetness of roasted garlic makes this recipe a tasty exception.

INGREDIENTS

3 pounds very ripe plum tomatoes, halved lengthwise

¼ cup extra virgin olive oil, plus more as needed

5 large garlic cloves

Salt and black pepper, to taste

Handful of basil leaves

1 Preheat the oven to 350°F. Place the tomatoes on a large parchment-lined baking sheet and drizzle with the olive oil. Using your fingers, mix well to ensure an even coating. Arrange the tomatoes cut side down, put the sheet on the center rack, lower the temperature to 325°F, and roast for 1 hour.

2 After 1 hour, remove the baking sheet, place the garlic in a small bowl, and drizzle with enough oil to lightly coat them. Add the garlic to the baking sheet and roast for another 30 minutes. Remove from the oven, season with salt and pepper, and let cool. Once cool enough to handle, remove the skins from the garlic cloves.

3 Place the roasted tomatoes, garlic, and basil leaves in a blender or food processor and puree until smooth. When ready to serve, transfer to a medium saucepan and cook over medium heat until gently bubbling.

Tomato and Eggplant Sauce alla Norma

YIELD: 4 SERVINGS • ACTIVE TIME: 40 MINUTES
TOTAL TIME: 1½ HOURS

From Sicily's ancient port city of Catania, this traditional sauce features a trifecta of the island's renowned ingredients: tomatoes, eggplant, and ricotta, which perfectly balances out the natural acidity in the tomatoes.

1 If the centers of the eggplants are overly seedy or spongy, remove those sections, as they will not help the texture and flavor of the sauce. Cut the eggplant quarters into 1-inch cubes, put in a colander, and sprinkle with 2 tablespoons of salt. Let drain for 30 minutes, and then thoroughly pat the cubes dry with paper towels.

2 Preheat the oven to 400°F. Place the eggplant cubes in a large baking pan, add the olive oil, and, using your hands, toss the eggplant and oil together until all the cubes are evenly coated. Spread the cubes into an even layer, place the pan on the center rack and roast, gently stirring twice during roasting, until they are tender and golden brown, about 25 minutes. Remove from the oven and set aside.

3 When ready to serve, place the eggplant cubes, tomato sauce, ricotta cheese, and basil in a large saucepan, stir to combine, and cook over medium heat until heated through. Season with salt and pepper before serving.

INGREDIENTS

2 medium, firm eggplants, peeled and quartered

2 tablespoons salt, plus more to taste

5 tablespoons extra virgin olive oil

5 cups Classic Fresh Tomato Sauce (see page 51)

1 cup ricotta cheese

Freshly ground black pepper, to taste

Arrabbiata

YIELD: 4 SERVINGS • ACTIVE TIME: 10 MINUTES
TOTAL TIME: 25 MINUTES

Arrabbiata translates to "angry," and this spicy sauce is sure to get your taste buds agitated—in a good way.

INGREDIENTS

2 tablespoons extra virgin olive oil

3 garlic cloves, crushed

2 dried chilies, chopped

1 (28 oz.) can of peeled San Marzano tomatoes

Handful of parsley, leaves removed and chopped

Salt and black pepper, to taste

1 Heat a large, deep skillet over low heat for 1 to 2 minutes. Add the olive oil, garlic, and chilies, raise the heat to medium-low, and cook until the garlic begins to turn golden, 1 to 2 minutes. Remove the garlic and as much of the chilies as possible and discard them, then add the tomatoes, breaking them up with your hands as you add them to the skillet (also add any liquid from the can). Raise the heat to medium-high and bring to a boil. Reduce the heat to medium-low and cook, while stirring occasionally, until the sauce is thick and the oil has risen to the surface, about 20 minutes.

2 Add the parsley and season with salt and pepper before serving.

Bolognese Sauce

**YIELD: 10 SERVINGS • ACTIVE TIME: 20 MINUTES
TOTAL TIME: 4½ HOURS**

Recipes for this rich meat sauce from the beautiful city of Bologna often include carrots; however, to enhance the sauce's savory flavor, it is better to omit them. The natural sugars of the carrots throw off the balance of the ingredients, making the sauce too sweet.

1 Heat a large heavy-bottomed pot over medium-low heat for 2 to 3 minutes. Add the olive oil and turn the heat up to medium-high. Heat the oil for a couple of minutes, then add the onion, celery, and a couple of pinches of salt, and stir. When the vegetables begin to sizzle, lower the heat to low, cover, and cook for 30 minutes, while stirring occasionally.

2 Raise the heat to medium-high and add the ground meat. With a potato masher or wooden spoon, press down on it to break up any large chunks. When the meat has turned a grayish brown and there is no pink remaining, add the milk. Continue cooking, while stirring occasionally, until the milk has completely evaporated.

3 Add the tomatoes, bay leaves, cloves, and a few pinches of salt, stir, and bring to a boil. Reduce the heat to low and cook, uncovered, for 4 hours, stirring every 30 minutes or so. You should see a gentle bubbling in the pot. You'll know the sauce is done when it has visibly thickened and the fat has separated. Discard the bay leaves before serving.

INGREDIENTS

3 tablespoons extra virgin olive oil

1 medium yellow onion, grated

2 celery stalks and fronds, grated

Salt, to taste

2 pounds ground meat (blend of pork, veal, and beef)

2 cups whole milk

2 (28 oz.) cans of peeled whole San Marzano tomatoes, pureed

2 bay leaves

7 cloves or 1 teaspoon ground cloves

Signora Sofia's Spiced Pork Sauce

**YIELD: 6 TO 8 SERVINGS • ACTIVE TIME: 20 MINUTES
TOTAL TIME: 1½ HOURS**

The kind of aromatic meat sauce for which ridged pasta such as penne was created, as it allows the sauce to adhere to each individual piece.

INGREDIENTS

6 tablespoons butter

1 medium yellow onion, grated

2 celery stalks, grated

Salt, to taste

1½ pounds ground pork

1 cup milk

5 cloves or ½ teaspoon ground cloves

1 cup chicken broth

2 tablespoons tomato paste

2 bay leaves

6 sage leaves

1 Heat a large heavy-bottomed pot over medium-low heat for 2 to 3 minutes. Add half of the butter and raise the heat to medium-high. When it's melted, add the onion, celery, and a couple pinches of salt and stir to combine. When the mixture starts to sizzle, reduce the heat to low, cover, and cook, while stirring occasionally, until the vegetables are very soft, about 30 minutes.

2 Add the ground pork to the pot and raise the heat to medium-high. Use a wooden spoon to break up the meat and mix it with the vegetables. Add a couple pinches of salt and mix well. When the meat has turned a grayish brown, add the milk. Continue cooking, while stirring occasionally, until the milk has completely evaporated, about 10 minutes.

3 Add the cloves, cook for 2 minutes, and then add the broth. Add the tomato paste and bay leaves, and bring to a boil. Adjust the heat to low, cover, and simmer for 45 minutes, stirring occasionally. You'll know the sauce is done when the fat has separated and is bubbling on the surface. Remove the bay leaf from the sauce and discard.

4 When the sauce is ready, melt the remaining butter in a small skillet over medium-low heat. Once it starts to bubble, add the sage leaves. Cook for a few minutes, until the leaves lightly crisp up and darken in color. Do not allow the butter to brown; you want to cook it just enough so that the sage leaves release their oil into the butter. Discard the sage, pour the butter into the meat sauce, and mix very well. Use or cool, transfer to an airtight container, and refrigerate for 3 days or freeze for up to 3 months.

Browned Butter and Sage Sauce

YIELD: 4 SERVINGS • ACTIVE TIME: 5 MINUTES
TOTAL TIME: 10 MINUTES

While piney and aromatic sage is the star in this classic pan sauce, the foundation provided by the toasty flavor of the browned butter is what allows it to shine.

INGREDIENTS

6 tablespoons unsalted butter, cut into small pieces

8 fresh sage leaves

Salt and black pepper, to taste

1 Heat a large skillet over medium-low heat for 2 to 3 minutes, and then add the butter. Raise the heat to medium and, once the butter melts and stops foaming, add the sage leaves.

2 Cook, while stirring occasionally, until the butter begins to brown on the bottom and the sage leaves become crispy. You will need to be very attentive during this step, as butter can burn in a blink of an eye. You want to make sure the sage is sizzling very gently so that it gets nice and crisp. Remove the pan from heat once the sage leaves are done, season with salt and pepper, remove the sage leaves from the butter, and reserve for a garnish.

Basil Pesto

YIELD: 4 SERVINGS • ACTIVE TIME: 25 MINUTES
TOTAL TIME: 25 MINUTES

The seaside region of Liguria has made many delectable contributions to Italian cooking, including focaccia. But this simple pesto is the most famous of them all.

1 Heat a small skillet over low heat for 1 minute. Add the nuts and cook, while stirring frequently, until either they begin to give off a toasty fragrance (if using walnuts), or until they become lightly golden brown (if using pine nuts), approximately 2 to 3 minutes. Transfer to a plate to cool.

2 Place the nuts, garlic, and salt in a food processor or blender and pulse until crushed and crumbly looking. Add the basil and pulse until finely minced. Transfer the mixture to a medium bowl and add the oil in a thin stream as you quickly whisk it in. Do not add the oil to the food processor or blender, as the oil becomes bitter when processed.

3 Add the cheeses, season with salt and pepper, and stir to thoroughly combine. Use or store in an airtight container, covered with a thin film of olive oil, in the refrigerator for up to 3 months.

INGREDIENTS

¼ cup toasted walnuts or pine nuts

2 large garlic cloves garlic, peeled

Sea salt and black pepper, to taste

2 cups basil, tightly packed

½ cup extra virgin olive oil

¼ cup pecorino Romano cheese, grated

¼ cup Parmesan cheese, grated

Chipotle and Pistachio Pesto

YIELD: 4 SERVINGS • ACTIVE TIME: 15 MINUTES
TOTAL TIME: 30 MINUTES

This sauce, as you might expect, is robust and needs to be paired with a hefty shape. Trofie (see pages 40–41), a traditional pasta from the northwestern region of Liguria, is a good choice; the creases on their surface zealously hold onto the sauce.

INGREDIENTS

4 canned chipotle peppers in adobo sauce, seeds removed

3 garlic cloves, peeled

⅔ cup salted pistachios, shelled

⅓ cup grapeseed oil

1 cup Manchego cheese, freshly grated

Salt, to taste

1 Place the chipotles and garlic in a food processor or blender and puree until smooth. Add the pistachios and pulse 5 or 6 times until slightly crushed. Transfer the mixture to a medium bowl and add the oil in a slow, steady stream while whisking continuously.

2 Add the Manchego, season with salt, and stir to combine.

Roasted Red Pepper, Creamy Corn, and Herb Sauce

YIELD: 4 SERVINGS • ACTIVE TIME: 30 MINUTES
TOTAL TIME: ABOUT 1 HOUR

This Mexican-inspired pasta sauce celebrates the bounty of a happy summer garden brimming with fresh red peppers, corn, parsley, and cilantro.

1 Preheat the oven to 500°F and then turn on the broiler. Place a wire rack on top of a parchment-lined baking sheet and set the peppers on top. Broil the peppers, while turning occasionally, until their skins are black and charred. Remove the peppers from the oven, place them in a mixing bowl, and cover it with a kitchen towel. When they are cool enough to handle, peel off the skin, discard the stems and seeds, and chop.

2 Heat a large skillet over medium-low heat for 2 to 3 minutes. Add the butter and heat for 1 to 2 minutes and then add scallions and a couple pinches of salt. Stir and cook until soft but not brown, 3 to 4 minutes. Add $\frac{2}{3}$ of the corn kernels, a couple more pinches of salt, and a pinch of ancho chili powder and stir. Cook until the kernels become soft, about 4 minutes, then remove from heat and let cool for 10 minutes. Transfer to a food processor and pulse to create a rough puree.

3 Heat a separate skillet over medium heat for 2 to 3 minutes. Add the olive oil and heat for 1 to 2 minutes. Add the peppers and the remaining corn, season with salt and pepper, and stir. Raise the heat to medium-high and cook for 5 to 6

INGREDIENTS

2 large red bell peppers

2 tablespoons unsalted butter

5 scallions, trimmed and thinly sliced

Salt and black pepper, to taste

Kernels from 4 ears of corn

Ground ancho chili powder, to taste

2 tablespoons extra virgin olive oil

2 handfuls of fresh parsley, minced

2 handfuls of fresh cilantro, minced

¼ cup heavy cream

¾ cup Cotija cheese, crumbled

minutes, or until the corn begins turning golden brown. Add half of the parsley and cilantro, stir to combine, and cook for 30 seconds.

4 Add the roughly pureed corn mixture and the cream, stir, and reduce the heat to low. Season with salt, pepper, and ancho chili powder and bring to a gentle simmer. Remove and cover until ready to serve. When ready to serve, top with the crumbled Cotija and the remaining parsley and cilantro.

Roasted Poblano Pepper Sauce

YIELD: 4 SERVINGS • ACTIVE TIME: 1 HOUR
TOTAL TIME: 1½ HOURS

This recipe fuses the subtle smoky quality of roasted poblanos, the sweetness of corn and caramelized onions, and the soothing silkiness of crema. This strategic union will enable you to enjoy the dish's zestiness without any fears of discomfort.

INGREDIENTS

3 poblano peppers

3 tablespoons extra virgin olive oil, plus more as needed

2 large Vidalia onions, halved and thinly sliced

Kernels from 3 ears of corn

Salt and black pepper, to taste

1 cup Mexican crema

¾ cup Manchego cheese, grated

Water or milk, as needed

1 Preheat the oven to 450°F. Place the poblanos on a parchment-lined baking sheet and place it on the center rack of the oven. Bake, while turning the peppers 3 to 4 times to promote even roasting, until the skins are completely wrinkled and charred, about 25 to 30 minutes. Remove from the oven, transfer the peppers to a mixing bowl, and cover with a kitchen towel. When they are cool enough to handle, remove the skin, seeds, and stems and cut into quarters.

2 Heat a large, deep skillet over low heat for 2 to 3 minutes. Add the 3 tablespoons of the olive oil and heat for a couple of minutes. Raise the heat to medium-low, add the onions and a couple pinches of salt, and cook until the onions are brown and very soft, about 45 minutes, while stirring occasionally. Transfer ½ cup of the cooked onions to a small bowl and set aside.

3 Add the corn and a couple pinches of salt to the onions remaining in the skillet. If the pan looks really dry, add another tablespoon of olive oil. Increase the heat to medium, and cook until the corn starts to brown, about 10 minutes. Transfer the mixture to a bowl.

4 While the corn is cooking, put the poblanos, the reserved caramelized onions, Mexican crema, Manchego, and 3 to 4 pinches of salt in a food processor or blender and puree until smooth. Add 1 to 2 tablespoons of water or milk if the mixture seems too thick.

5 Reheat the skillet over medium-low heat. Add more olive oil and heat for 1 or 2 minutes. Add the poblano puree and cook until heated through. Season to taste and cover. When serving, add to pasta, toss to coat, and top with the onion-and-corn mixture.

Rose Sauce

Thick, creamy, and comforting, this sauce has never met a child it couldn't mesmerize. Reducing the cream is essential to this recipe, as it adds an even greater level of flavor and richness to the sauce.

INGREDIENTS

4 pounds very ripe plum tomatoes, concasse (see page 50) and chopped

4 tablespoons unsalted butter

½ white or Vidalia onion, cut into quarters

Salt and black pepper, to taste

1 teaspoon sugar (optional)

2 cups heavy cream

1 Place the tomatoes in a food processor or blender and puree until smooth.

2 Heat a medium saucepan over medium-low heat for 2 to 3 minutes. Add the butter and raise the heat to medium. Once it melts and stops foaming, add the onion and a pinch of salt and stir. When it begins to gently sizzle, adjust the heat to low, cover, and cook, while stirring occasionally, until the onion has softened, about 10 minutes.

3 Add the pureed tomatoes and a couple pinches of salt. If the tomatoes are not in season, add the sugar and stir. Bring to a boil, then reduce the heat to low and simmer for 20 minutes. Remove the onion pieces with a slotted spoon and discard.

4 As the tomato sauce cooks, add the cream to a small saucepan and cook over low heat until it has reduced by about half. Remove from heat. Once the tomato sauce has thickened, add the reduced cream, season with salt and pepper, and stir.

Smoked Salmon and Asparagus Sauce

YIELD: 4 SERVINGS • ACTIVE TIME: 20 MINUTES
TOTAL TIME: 3 HOURS AND 45 MINUTES

This particular jewel was developed by Florence Fabricant, the acclaimed long-time contributor to the *New York Times*. Pleasantly creamy and smoky, this sauce comes together quickly and is good enough to wow anyone who comes past your table.

INGREDIENTS

2 leeks, white and light green parts only, thinly sliced

4 oz. smoked salmon, sliced

¾ cup heavy cream

1 teaspoon fresh nutmeg, grated

1 pound asparagus, trimmed

2 tablespoons water

1½ tablespoons unsalted butter

Salt, to taste

1 Place the sliced leeks in a large bowl of water and swish them around with your hands to remove any dirt. Pour the leeks into a colander and rinse under cold water. Drain again and transfer to a kitchen towel to air-dry until needed.

2 Place the salmon in a small bowl and add the cream and nutmeg. Mix, cover, and marinate for 2 to 3 hours in a naturally cool place.

3 Place the asparagus in a microwave-safe dish and add the water. Cover with plastic wrap and microwave, 1 minute for thin asparagus and 1½ to 2 minutes for thick asparagus. Remove from the microwave and rinse under cold water. Drain and then pat dry. Cut each spear in half lengthwise and then cut them into ½-inch long pieces.

4 Heat a large skillet over medium-low heat for 2 to 3 minutes. Add the butter and raise the heat to medium-high. When it's melted, add all the asparagus pieces and a couple pinches of salt and stir. Cook, while stirring occasionally, until they just begin to turn golden, 4 to 5 minutes. Transfer them to a plate and cover with foil.

5 Add the leeks and a pinch of salt to the skillet, stir, and cover. Cook, while stirring occasionally, until they are soft and translucent, about 15 minutes. Add the asparagus and salmon-and-cream mixture and stir well. Reduce the heat to low and cook until heated through, about 5 minutes.

Shrimp and Pistou Sauce

YIELD: 4 SERVINGS • ACTIVE TIME: 35 MINUTES
TOTAL TIME: 1 HOUR

Pistou, the recipe's flavor powerhouse, is an olive oil-based condiment from Provence. While traditional pistou is green and made predominantly from basil, garlic, and Parmesan, this version contains tomato paste for extra depth of flavor.

INGREDIENTS

1½ pounds medium to large shrimp, peeled and deveined

4 garlic cloves, peeled

5 tablespoons tomato paste

Salt and black pepper, to taste

½ cup Parmesan cheese, grated

2 handfuls of basil leaves, torn or cut into ribbons

6½ tablespoons extra virgin olive oil

3 cups Classic Fresh Tomato Sauce (see page 51)

½ cup water

1 Place the shrimp on a paper towel-lined plate to drain, as they will cook better when they are at room temperature.

2 Place the garlic, tomato paste, and a generous pinch of salt in a food processor or blender and pulse until well combined. Add the Parmesan and pulse until integrated. Add the basil and pulse for just a few seconds; you want to see pieces of the basil in the mixture—it shouldn't be a smooth puree. Transfer the mixture to a small bowl and whisk in 4 tablespoons of the olive oil until well combined. This is your pistou, which can be stored in the refrigerator for 1 week or in the freezer for up to 3 months.

3 Heat a large, deep skillet over medium heat for 2 to 3 minutes. Add the remaining olive oil and heat for 1 or 2 minutes. Gently pat the shrimp with a

paper towel to absorb as much surface moisture as possible and sprinkle with salt. When the surface of the oil begins to glisten, add the shrimp to the skillet in a single layer, making sure there is plenty of room between them. You will likely have to cook them in several batches. Sear the shrimp for 2 minutes on each side, then transfer to a warm plate and cover with aluminum foil.

4 Add the tomato sauce and water to the skillet and cook over medium-high heat until the sauce begins to bubble. Add the pistou, stir until well combined, and season with salt and pepper. Once the sauce starts bubbling, reduce heat to low, cover, and keep warm. When ready to serve, pour over the pasta and top with the cooked shrimp.

Sausage Ragù

YIELD: 4 SERVINGS • ACTIVE TIME: 20 MINUTES
TOTAL TIME: 2½ HOURS

This is a real stick-to-your-ribs kind of sauce, mostly because of the considerable fat content in sausage. It's the type of dish that nourishes both body and soul, especially after a day of gardening or hiking in the mountains.

1 Heat a Dutch oven over medium-low heat for 2 to 3 minutes. Add the olive oil and raise the heat to medium-high. Once it begins to glisten, add the sausage, onion, garlic, and paprika. Use a wooden spoon to crumble the sausage. Season with salt and pepper and cook, while stirring occasionally, for 10 minutes.

2 Add the thyme and the tomatoes with their juices. Bring to a boil, then reduce the heat to low and simmer for 2 hours. The sauce is done when it has visibly thickened and the fat has separated and is bubbling on the surface.

INGREDIENTS

3 tablespoons extra virgin olive oil

4 sweet Italian sausages, casings removed

1 small onion, minced

2 garlic cloves, thinly sliced

½ teaspoon paprika

Salt and black pepper, to taste

2 sprigs of fresh thyme

1 (28 oz.) can of peeled San Marzano tomatoes, crushed by hand

Lamb Ragù

YIELD: 6 TO 8 SERVINGS • ACTIVE TIME: 35 MINUTES
TOTAL TIME: ABOUT 3 HOURS

This sauce, which goes well with egg-based pasta, is quite easy to make, it just requires time to simmer. Use that down time to enjoy a glass (or two) of your favorite Bordeaux or Rioja.

INGREDIENTS

2 tablespoons extra virgin olive oil

2 small onions, minced

2 pale green celery stalks, minced

Salt and pepper, to taste

2 pounds ground lamb

1 cup dry red wine

3 to 4 small sprigs of thyme, leaves removed and minced

2 small sprigs of fresh marjoram, minced

1 small dried chili pepper

2 (28 oz.) cans of peeled San Marzano tomatoes, crushed by hand

1 Heat a Dutch oven over medium-low heat for 2 to 3 minutes. Add the olive oil and raise the heat to medium-high. After 1 minute, add the onions, celery, and a couple pinches of salt and stir to combine. When the mixture starts to sizzle, reduce the heat to low, cover, and cook, while stirring occasionally, until the vegetables are very soft and slightly dark, about 30 minutes.

2 Add the lamb to the pot and cook, breaking it apart with a wooden spoon, until it is no longer pink. Raise the heat to medium-high, add the wine and cook for 5 minutes. Add the thyme, marjoram, and chili, stir, and cook for 2 minutes. Add the tomatoes and their juices, season with salt and pepper, stir, and bring to a boil. Reduce the heat to medium-low so that the sauce gently simmers. Cover and cook, while stirring occasionally, for 2 hours. You'll know the sauce is done when it has visibly thickened and the fat has separated and is bubbling on the surface.

Broccoli Rabe and Ham Sauce

YIELD: 4 SERVINGS • ACTIVE TIME: 25 MINUTES
TOTAL TIME: 40 MINUTES

This is a somewhat gussied-up version of an old classic from Southern Italy. To eliminate the bitterness for which broccoli rabe is known, make sure to aggressively trim it to just the florets, the smaller (and more tender) leaves, and the thinnest stems.

1 Bring 8 cups of water to a boil in a large saucepan. Once it's boiling, add the salt and stir. Add the broccoli rabe and boil for 6 minutes. Drain and rinse under cold water. Squeeze to remove excess water and then chop.

2 Heat a large skillet over low heat for 2 to 3 minutes. Add the olive oil and raise the heat to medium. Once the oil begins to glisten, add the onion, garlic, and a pinch of salt and stir. Cook until the onion turns translucent, about 4 to 5 minutes. Add the capers and ham and cook, while stirring frequently, until the mixture becomes very soft, 5 to 6 minutes. Add the broccoli rabe and a couple pinches of salt, stir well to combine, and cook for another 5 minutes.

INGREDIENTS

2 tablespoons salt, plus more to taste

1½ pounds broccoli rabe, florets, small leaves, and thin stems only

4 tablespoons extra virgin olive oil

1 small yellow onion, minced

3 garlic cloves, thinly sliced

1 tablespoon nonpareil capers, rinsed

4 oz. sliced ham, julienned

Béchamel Sauce

Which country is responsible for the existence of this sauce has long been a topic of debate between Italy and France, but we're certain about this: when properly prepared, béchamel adds a creamy texture, a light buttery taste, and moisture to baked dishes.

INGREDIENTS

8 tablespoons (1 stick) unsalted butter

½ cup all-purpose flour

4 cups whole milk

½ teaspoon nutmeg, grated

Salt and freshly ground white pepper, to taste

1 Melt the butter in a medium saucepan over medium heat, making sure it does not brown. Add the flour all at once and quickly whisk until the mixture becomes velvety smooth. Cook, while whisking constantly, for 5 minutes, until the mixture stops foaming and turns golden.

2 Pour in ½ cup of the milk and whisk vigorously until you've loosened the mixture. Add the rest of the milk and cook, while whisking constantly. Within minutes the mixture will start to thicken. Add the nutmeg and season with salt and pepper. Stir to combine and use immediately or let cool, cover, and refrigerate for up to 2 days. Bring back to room temperature before using.

> **TIP:** BÉCHAMEL IS ALSO THE PERFECT SAUCE TO INJECT SOME LIFE INTO LEFTOVER PASTA THAT UTILIZES A TOMATO-BASED SAUCE.

Italian Noodles

For many, noodles are synonymous with Italian food. Thanks to dishes like Spaghetti alla Carbonara (see pages 86–87) and Penne alla Vodka (see pages 106–107), Italy's fingerprints are on pasta makers and saucepans all over the world.

While this chapter does feature those aforementioned classics, we feel we'd be letting you down if we didn't do something to expand your horizons. With that task before us, we've imported a few preparations that are beloved in Italy but, for whatever reason, haven't accompanied their comrades on the journey around the world. From the Linguine in Aromatic Walnut Sauce (see pages 98–99) to Bucatini all'Amatriciana (see pages 96–97), you'll soon see that the Old Country has no shortage of dishes that will delight the family.

Spaghetti alla Carbonara

YIELD: 4 SERVINGS • ACTIVE TIME: 15 MINUTES
TOTAL TIME: 30 MINUTES

Beloved for its satisfying savory flavor, carbonara develops a cream-like sauce when eggs and cheese are tossed with the hot spaghetti.

1 Put a large pot of water on to boil. While the water comes to a boil, heat a medium skillet over medium-low heat for 2 to 3 minutes. Add 2 tablespoons of the olive oil and let it warm for a couple of minutes. Raise the heat to medium, add the pancetta, and season with pepper. Cook, while stirring occasionally, until pancetta renders its fat and starts turning golden brown, about 4 to 5 minutes. Remove the skillet from heat and partially cover.

2 Place the eggs in a small bowl and whisk until thoroughly combined. Add the Parmesan, season with salt and pepper, and whisk until combined.

3 Once the water is boiling, add salt (1 tablespoon for every 4 cups of water) and stir. Add the pasta and cook 2 minutes short of the directed cooking time. The pasta should be soft but still very firm. Right before draining the pasta, reserve ¼ cup of the pasta water.

4 Return the pot to the stove, raise the heat to high, and add the remaining olive oil and the reserved pasta water. Add the drained pasta and toss. Remove the pot from heat, add the pancetta and the egg-and-Parmesan mixture, and toss to coat. Divide the pasta among four warm bowls, season with pepper, and top with additional Parmesan.

INGREDIENTS

2½ tablespoons extra virgin olive oil

4 oz. pancetta, diced

Salt and black pepper, to taste

2 large eggs at room temperature

¾ cup Parmesan cheese, grated, plus more for garnish

¾ pound spaghetti

Spaghetti alla Serena

YIELD: 4 SERVINGS • ACTIVE TIME: 45 MINUTES
TOTAL TIME: 1 HOUR AND 15 MINUTES

Though the lineage of this Midwestern classic is somewhat unclear, it provides a savory, filling, and completely accessible meal.

1 Place the wine in a small saucepan, bring to a boil, and cook until reduced by half, about 5 minutes. Remove pan from the stove and set aside.

2 Heat a large skillet over medium-low heat for 2 to 3 minutes and then add 2 tablespoons of the butter. Once it has melted and stopped foaming, raise the heat to medium-high, add half of the mushrooms and a pinch of salt, and cook, while stirring occasionally, until the mushrooms have softened and browned slightly, about 6 to 8 minutes. Transfer to a warm bowl and cover with aluminum foil. Add 2 more tablespoons of the butter to the same pan, add the remaining mushrooms and another pinch of salt, and repeat.

3 Add the olive oil, raise the heat to medium, and cook for 1 minute. Add the onion and cook until it becomes translucent, about 5 minutes. Add the bell pepper and cook until tender, 8 to 10 minutes. Raise the heat to medium-high and cook until the edges of the bell pepper begin to color, 4 to 5 minutes.

4 Return the mushrooms to the skillet and stir to combine. Add the reduced wine and the milk, bring to a boil, and reduce the heat to low. Add the remaining butter and the Gruyère and stir until melted. Add the chicken and parsley, season with salt and pepper, and cook while stirring occasionally, until the chicken is heated through.

INGREDIENTS

²/₃ cup Madeira wine

8½ tablespoons unsalted butter

1 pound cremini mushrooms,
cleaned and quartered

Salt and freshly ground white
pepper, to taste

2 tablespoons extra virgin olive oil

1 small yellow onion, grated

1 red bell pepper, seeded
and cut into thin strips

1 cup whole milk

6 oz. Gruyère cheese, grated

2 cups cooked
chicken breast, shredded

Handful of fresh parsley leaves,
chopped, plus more for garnish

¾ pound spaghetti

Parmesan cheese,
grated, for garnish

5 Bring a pot of salted water (1 tablespoon of salt for every 4 cups water) to boil, add the pasta, and cook 1 minute short of the directed time. Reserve ½ cup of pasta water, drain, and return the pot to the stove. Add reserved pasta water, turn heat to high, add the pasta, and cook until water is absorbed. Transfer pasta to skillet and toss until combined. Season to taste and garnish with additional parsley and Parmesan before serving.

Spaghetti with Fontina Sauce

**YIELD: 4 SERVINGS • ACTIVE TIME: 40 MINUTES
TOTAL TIME: 1½ HOURS**

While the sauce is delicious, what makes this dish so satisfying is the balance between the nutty-buttery quality of the sauce and the intense flavor of the roasted vegetables.

1 Preheat the oven to 450°F. Place the cauliflower and 2 tablespoons of the olive oil in a large bowl and toss to coat. Transfer to a baking pan, season with salt and pepper, cover the pan with foil, and then place in the oven. Cook for 15 minutes, remove from oven, and use a spatula to turn the cauliflower over. Return to the oven uncovered, lower the temperature to 400°F, and cook until soft and the edges are browned, about 40 minutes.

2 While the cauliflower is roasting, place the mushrooms in the large bowl with 2 tablespoons of the olive oil and toss to coat. Transfer to a parchment-lined baking sheet, season with salt and pepper, and sprinkle with the thyme. Place in the 400°F oven, cook for 15 minutes, and remove from oven. Carefully drain the liquid, return to the oven, and cook until soft and lightly browned, about 25 minutes.

3 Heat a large skillet over medium-low heat for 2 to 3 minutes. Add 2 tablespoons of the oil and raise the heat to medium. Add the bacon and cook until it turns golden and crisp, 8 to 10 minutes. Transfer it to a small bowl and set aside.

4 Add the onion, season with salt, and raise the heat to medium-high. Cook,

INGREDIENTS

Florets from 1 head of cauliflower

6½ tablespoons extra virgin olive oil

Salt and black pepper, to taste

1 pound cremini mushrooms, stemmed and roughly chopped

3 sprigs of thyme, leaves removed

6 oz. bacon, chopped into ½-inch pieces

1 large yellow onion, grated

½ cup chicken broth

4 oz. Fontina cheese, grated

¾ cup heavy cream

½ tablespoon Worcestershire sauce

¾ pound pasta

Parsley, chopped, for garnish

while stirring, until the onion starts to sizzle. Reduce the heat to low, cover, and cook, while stirring occasionally, until the onion becomes very soft, about 15 minutes. Raise the heat to medium-high, add the broth, cheese, and cream, and stir until the mixture is bubbly. Stir in the Worcestershire sauce, remove the skillet from heat, and cover to keep warm.

5 Bring a pot of salted water (1 tablespoon of salt for every 4 cups water) to boil, add the pasta, and cook 2 minutes short of the directed time. Reserve ¼ cup of pasta water, drain, and return the pot to the stove. Add reserved pasta water and the remaining olive oil, raise heat to high, add the pasta, and cook until water is absorbed. Add the contents of the skillet and cook, while stirring, for 1 to 2 minutes. Top with roasted vegetables and bacon bits and garnish with parsley.

Spaghetti with Calamari Fra Diavolo

YIELD: 6 SERVINGS • ACTIVE TIME: 40 MINUTES
TOTAL TIME: 1 HOUR

This recipe replaces the shrimp that are traditionally used in a fra diavolo sauce with tender rings and tentacles of baby squid, giving the dish a springy—but not chewy—texture.

1 Place the wine in a small saucepan, bring to a boil, and cook until reduced by half, about 5 minutes. Remove pan from the stove and set aside.

2 Wash the squid thoroughly and transfer to a paper towel-lined plate to drain. Blot the squid with paper towels to absorb as much surface moisture as possible.

3 Heat a large, deep skillet over medium heat for 2 to 3 minutes. Add 3 tablespoons of the olive oil, the garlic, half of the red pepper flakes, and a pinch of salt and cook for 2 to 3 minutes. Once the garlic begins to sizzle, raise the heat to medium-high and add the squid, anchovies, and half of the parsley. Cook, while stirring occasionally, until the anchovies dissolve and the calamari turns golden, about 5 minutes. Add the reduced wine and continue to cook until the mixture is reduced by a third, about 5 minutes. Add the tomatoes, the broth or clam juice, and the remaining red pepper flakes, season with salt, and stir. Bring to a boil, then reduce the heat to medium-low and simmer until the sauce is slightly thickened, about 20 minutes.

4 Bring a pot of salted water (1 tablespoon of salt for every 4 cups water) to boil, add the pasta, and cook 2 minutes short of the directed time. Reserve ¼ cup of pasta water, drain, and return the pot to the stove. Add reserved pasta water and remaining olive oil, turn heat to high, add the pasta, and cook until water is absorbed. Add the contents of the skillet and toss continuously for 2 minutes. Season to taste and garnish with the remaining parsley and the oregano before serving.

INGREDIENTS

1 cup dry red wine

2 pounds squid, bodies cut into rings, tentacles halved lengthwise

3½ tablespoons extra virgin olive oil

4 garlic cloves, minced

1 teaspoon red pepper flakes

Salt, to taste

3 oil-packed anchovy fillets

2 handfuls of parsley, chopped

1 (28 oz.) can of peeled whole plum tomatoes, pureed

½ cup fish broth or clam juice

1 pound spaghetti

Oregano, chopped, for garnish

Spaghetti alla Gricia

**YIELD: 4 SERVINGS • ACTIVE TIME: 10 MINUTES
TOTAL TIME: 30 MINUTES**

Gricia is a classic sauce that is particularly popular in Rome. As it consists of just three primary ingredients, you want to make sure you don't skimp on quality while shopping.

Heat a large, deep skillet over medium-low heat for 2 to 3 minutes. Add the guanciale, raise the heat to medium, and cook, while stirring occasionally, until the fat starts to render and the edges start to brown, about 20 minutes. Add the pepper, stir, and remove the skillet from heat.

Bring a pot of salted water (1 tablespoon of salt for every 4 cups water) to boil, add the pasta, and cook 1 minute less than the directed time. Reserve ⅓ cup of pasta water, drain, and return the pot to the stove. Add reserved pasta water and the olive oil, raise heat to high, add the pasta, and toss. Add the guanciale, its rendered fat, and the pecorino and cook, while tossing, for 2 minutes. Season with salt and pepper and garnish with additional pecorino.

INGREDIENTS

Bucatini all'Amatriciana

YIELD: 4 SERVINGS • ACTIVE TIME: 15 MINUTES
TOTAL TIME: 45 MINUTES

Many opinions abound about whether it is guanciale or pancetta, pecorino or Parmesan that make an Amatriciana authentic, but there's no argument that every approximation of this dish is incredibly satisfying.

1 Bring a large pot of water to a boil. Heat a large, deep skillet large over medium-low heat for 2 to 3 minutes, add the olive oil, and warm for 2 minutes. Raise the heat to medium and add the guanciale or pancetta and chilies. Cook until the meat turns a light golden color, 5 to 6 minutes. Transfer the meat to a small dish and set aside.

2 Bring a pot of salted water to boil, add salt (1 tablespoon for every 4 cups water), and stir. Add the bucatini and cook 2 minutes less than the directed cooking time.

3 While the pasta is cooking, raise the heat under the skillet to medium-high and add the wine. Scrape up all the browned bits stuck to bottom of the pan with a wooden spoon. Cook for 5 minutes, add the tomatoes and sugar, and season with salt and pepper. Cook for 10 minutes, adding a few spoonfuls of pasta water if the sauce looks too thick.

4 Drain the pasta while reserving ¼ cup of the water. Return the pot to the stove. Add reserved pasta water, raise heat to high, add the pasta, drizzle with olive oil, and toss for 1 minute. Transfer pasta to skillet, sprinkle with pecorino and reserved guanciale or pancetta, and cook, while tossing, for 2 minutes. Season with salt and pepper and garnish with parsley and additional pecorino.

INGREDIENTS

1 tablespoon extra virgin olive oil, plus more for drizzling

4 oz. guanciale or pancetta, sliced

2 dried red chilies, chopped

Salt and black pepper, to taste

¾ pound bucatini

½ cup dry white wine

2½ pounds very ripe plum tomatoes, concasse (see page 50) and chopped

2 pinches of sugar

½ cup pecorino Romano, grated

Handful of parsley, chopped, for garnish

TIP: FOR A MILDER VERSION, REMOVE THE SEEDS OF THE CHILI PEPPERS BEFORE USING.

INGREDIENTS

1 cup day-old country bread, cubed

1 cup walnuts

1 garlic clove, thinly sliced

¼ cup bread crumbs

Handful of parsley, chopped

2 sprigs of marjoram,
leaves removed and chopped

3 tablespoons walnut oil

3 tablespoons heavy cream

5 tablespoons unsalted butter
at room temperature

Salt, to taste

¾ pound linguine

Gorgonzola, crumbled, for garnish

Linguine in Aromatic Walnut Sauce

YIELD: 4 SERVINGS • ACTIVE TIME: 20 MINUTES
TOTAL TIME: 50 MINUTES

Thick and creamy, this decadent sauce hails from the herb-laden hills of Liguria in Northwestern Italy. As it is not often seen on the menu in Italian restaurants, it should be indulged in as often as possible.

1 Place the bread cubes in a small bowl, cover with warm water, and let soak for 30 minutes. Drain, tightly squeeze the bread to remove as much water as possible, and set aside.

2 Bring a small saucepan of water to a boil, add the walnuts, cook for 2 minutes, drain, and let cool. When cool enough to handle, rub off their skins and place on paper towels to dry. Place in a small resealable bag and break them up with a rolling pin. Transfer to a small bowl.

3 Place the bread cubes, walnuts, garlic, bread crumbs, parsley, and half the marjoram in a food processor or blender. Pulse until you have a smooth paste. Transfer to a medium bowl, add the walnut oil, and whisk until it is thoroughly incorporated. Add the cream, 3 tablespoons of the butter, season with salt, and whisk until well combined.

4 Bring a pot of salted water (1 tablespoon of salt for every 4 cups water) to boil, add the pasta, and cook 2 minutes less than the directed time. Reserve ¼ cup of pasta water, drain, and return the pot to the stove. Add the remaining butter and reserved pasta water, raise heat to high, add the pasta, and toss until the water is absorbed. Add the walnut sauce and cook, while stirring, for 1 to 2 minutes. Garnish with the remaining marjoram and the Gorgonzola before serving.

Fettuccine in Puttanesca Sauce

YIELD: 4 SERVINGS • ACTIVE TIME: 15 MINUTES
TOTAL TIME: 30 MINUTES

This spicy dish is reputed to have been invented by "ladies of the night" who wanted to lure unwitting customers into their lairs. Take just one whiff of this aromatic sauce and the legend will seem more than plausible.

INGREDIENTS

½ cup extra virgin olive oil

3 garlic cloves, minced

1 (28 oz.) can of peeled San Marzano tomatoes, crushed by hand

½ pound black olives, pitted

¼ cup nonpareil capers

5 oil-packed anchovy fillets or 2 whole salt-packed anchovies

1 teaspoon red pepper flakes

Salt and black pepper, to taste

¾ pound fettuccine

Handful of parsley, chopped, for garnish

Parmesan, grated, for garnish

1 Place a large, deep skillet over low heat for 2 minutes. Add the olive oil and garlic and increase the heat to medium-low. Cook the garlic until it begins to sizzle gently, add the tomatoes and their juice, olives, capers, and anchovies and stir while pressing down on the anchovies to break them up. Add the red pepper flakes, season with salt and pepper, stir to combine, and raise the heat to medium. Simmer, while stirring occasionally, until the sauce thickens slightly, about 10 minutes. Remove from heat and cover to keep warm.

2 Bring a pot of salted water (1 tablespoon of salt for every 4 cups water) to boil, add the pasta, and cook 2 minutes short of the directed time. Reserve ¼ cup of pasta water, drain, and return the pot to the stove. Add reserved pasta water, turn heat to high, add the pasta, and cook until water is absorbed. Add the sauce and cook, while stirring, for 1 to 2 minutes. Season with pepper and garnish with the parsley and Parmesan before serving.

Orecchiette with Arugula and Potatoes

YIELD: 4 SERVINGS • ACTIVE TIME: 20 MINUTES
TOTAL TIME: 30 MINUTES

The ideal dish for a weeknight dinner: flavorful, quick, and the perfect partner for a simple salad.

1 Heat a large, deep skillet over low heat for 2 to 3 minutes, add the 6 tablespoons of olive oil, garlic, capers, olives, and cayenne, and cook, while stirring occasionally, for 5 minutes. When the garlic is lightly golden, discard it and remove the skillet from heat.

2 Bring a pot of salted water (1 tablespoon of salt for every 4 cups water) to boil and add the potatoes. When the water begins to boil again, add the pasta and cook according to manufacturer's instructions. Add the arugula 1 minute prior to draining the pasta. Reserve ½ cup of pasta water, drain, and return the pot to the stove.

3 Place the skillet containing the sauce over medium-high heat. Add reserved pasta water to the pot, turn heat to high and add the pasta, potatoes, arugula, and the remaining olive oil. Toss until water is absorbed. Transfer to the skillet and cook, while tossing, for 2 minutes. Add the pecorino and toss until combined. Season with salt and pepper and garnish with additional pecorino before serving.

INGREDIENTS

6 tablespoons extra virgin olive oil, plus 1 teaspoon

2 garlic cloves, halved

1 teaspoon nonpareil capers, rinsed, drained, and minced

½ cup green olives, pitted and minced

⅛ teaspoon cayenne pepper

2 large russet potatoes, peeled and cubed

Salt and black pepper, to taste

¾ pound orecchiette, homemade (see pages 34–35) or store-bought

½ pound baby arugula

¼ cup pecorino Romano, grated, plus more for garnish

Penne with Clams and Calamari

**YIELD: 4 SERVINGS • ACTIVE TIME: 25 MINUTES
TOTAL TIME: 30 MINUTES**

American renditions of this dish often feature a heavy tomato sauce. The Italian version featured here includes tomatoes only for a splash of color and a hint of flavor so that the true star of this dish, the briny clams, can shine.

INGREDIENTS

¾ **pound squid bodies and tentacles, sliced**

Salt and black pepper, to taste

¼ **cup extra virgin olive oil, plus 1 teaspoon**

3 large plum tomatoes, concasse (see page 50) and chopped

2 garlic cloves, thinly sliced

3½ **pounds small hard-shell clams, scrubbed and rinsed**

¾ **pound penne**

2 handfuls of parsley, chopped, for garnish

1 Place the pieces of squid in a colander, rinse, and drain. Sprinkle with salt and pepper, toss, and set aside.

2 Bring a large pot of water to a boil to cook the pasta. As the water heats up, heat a large, deep skillet over medium-low heat for 2 to 3 minutes. Add the ¼ cup of olive oil, raise the heat to medium-high, and warm for 1 minute. Add the tomatoes, garlic, and squid, season with salt, and cook for 5 minutes. Add the clams and cook, while stirring occasionally, until a few begin to open. Remove from the heat and cover the skillet. While the pasta is cooking in Step 3, discard any clams that do not open.

3 Once the pasta water is boiling, add salt (1 tablespoon for every 4 cups water) and stir. Add the penne and cook 2 minutes less than the directed cooking time. Reserve ½ cup of the pasta water, drain, and return the pot to the stove. Raise the heat to high and add the remaining oil and the reserved pasta water. Add the pasta, toss, and then add the contents of the skillet. Cook, while tossing, for 2 minutes and garnish with the parsley before serving.

Penne alla Vodka

YIELD: 6 SERVINGS • ACTIVE TIME: 40 MINUTES
TOTAL TIME: 1 HOUR

Though its flavor is imperceptible, the vodka is key to this quintessential comfort food, as it brings out the flavors in tomatoes that are alcohol-soluble and otherwise inaccessible to the palate.

INGREDIENTS

4 to 6 oz. pancetta, diced

2½ tablespoons unsalted butter

3 shallots, minced

Salt, to taste

1 (28 oz.) can of peeled San Marzano tomatoes, puréed

1 teaspoon red pepper flakes

1 cup heavy cream

1 lb. penne

1/3 cup vodka at room temperature

1 cup Parmesan cheese, grated, plus more for garnish

2 handfuls of parsley, chopped, for garnish

Place a large skillet over medium-low heat for 2 to 3 minutes and then add the pancetta. Raise the heat to medium and cook, while stirring occasionally, until the pieces become crisp, 8 to 10 minutes. Transfer to a small bowl and set aside. Add 2 tablespoons of the butter to the skillet. Once it has melted and stopped foaming, add the shallots and a pinch of salt. Once the shallots begin to sizzle, reduce the heat to low, cover, and cook, while stirring occasionally, until soft, about 10 minutes.

Add the tomatoes and red pepper flakes, season with salt, and raise the heat to medium-high. Once the mixture begins to boil, reduce the heat to low, partially cover, and cook until the sauce slightly thickens, 15 to 20 minutes. Add the cream and heat through until the sauce gently bubbles. Remove from heat and cover.

Bring a pot of salted water (1 tablespoon of salt for every 4 cups water) to boil, add the pasta, and cook

2 minutes short of the directed time. Reserve ¼ cup of pasta water, drain, and return the pot to the stove. Add reserved pasta water, vodka, and remaining butter, turn heat to high, add the pasta, and cook until water is absorbed. Add the sauce and the Parmesan to the pot and toss for 2 minutes. Top with the pancetta and garnish with the parsley and additional Parmesan.

Kira's Garganelli with Cream, Ham, and Peas

YIELD: 4 SERVINGS • ACTIVE TIME: 10 MINUTES
TOTAL TIME: 40 MINUTES

The quartet of garganelli, cream, ham, and peas is legendary in the Emilia-Romagna region of Italy. If you're unable to track down this tubular pasta, turn to one of its twisted brethren, such as fusilli.

INGREDIENTS

1 tablespoon extra virgin olive oil

6 oz. thick-cut ham, cut into 1-inch pieces

4½ tablespoons unsalted butter

3 shallots, minced

Salt and white pepper, to taste

¾ pound garganelli, homemade (see page 43) or store-bought

1½ cups frozen peas

¾ cup heavy cream

1 teaspoon nutmeg, grated

Parmesan cheese, grated, for garnish

1 Heat a large, deep skillet over medium heat for 2 to 3 minutes. Add the olive oil and raise the heat to medium-high. Add the ham and cook until it turns golden brown and crisp, about 5 minutes. Transfer the ham to a small bowl and set aside.

2 Add 4 tablespoons of the butter to the skillet. Once it has melted and stopped foaming, add the shallots and a pinch of salt and reduce the heat to low. Cover, and cook, while stirring occasionally, until the shallots are very soft and golden brown, about 15 minutes.

3 While the shallots are cooking, bring a large pot of water to a boil. When it's boiling, add salt (1 tablespoon for every 4 cups water) and stir. Add the pasta, cook for 5 minutes, and then add the peas. Drain the pasta 2 minutes short of the directed cooking time, reserving ½ cup of the cooking water.

4 When the shallots are ready, add the cream and nutmeg and season with salt and pepper. Bring to a simmer, cook for 3 minutes, and then remove the skillet from heat.

5 After draining the pasta, return the empty pot to the stove. Add the remaining butter and reserved pasta water, raise the heat to high, add the drained pasta and peas, and toss. Add the contents of the skillet and cook, while tossing, for 2 minutes. Top with the ham and garnish with Parmesan before serving.

Pasta Primavera

**YIELD: 6 SERVINGS • ACTIVE TIME: 35 MINUTES
TOTAL TIME: 1 HOUR**

Supposedly invented by the chefs at New York's famed Le Cirque in the 1970s and a longtime favorite of the power lunch crowd, this delicious amalgam of fresh vegetables, crunchy panko, and rich cream will win over even the most finicky eaters.

1 Preheat the oven to 400°F. Heat a large skillet over medium-low heat for 2 to 3 minutes, then add 2 tablespoons of the butter. Once it has melted and stopped foaming, add the bread crumbs and cook, while stirring constantly, until they are dark golden brown, 4 to 5 minutes. Remove from heat, pour into a bowl, season with salt and pepper, and stir.

2 Place the zucchini and bell peppers in a large bowl, drizzle with 2 tablespoons of the oil, and toss until evenly coated. Transfer to a parchment-lined baking sheet and spread them out in a single layer. Add the carrots to the same large bowl, drizzle with the remaining oil, and toss until evenly coated. Transfer to another parchment-lined baking sheet and spread them out in a single layer. Place both baking sheets in the oven. Roast the zucchini and peppers, stirring once about halfway through, until softened and browned, 10 to 12 minutes. Roast the carrots, stirring once about halfway through, until fork-tender and lightly browned, 15 to 18 minutes. Remove from the oven, sprinkle with salt and pepper, mix well, and set aside.

3 While the vegetables are roasting, bring a large pot of water to a boil. Combine the cream, Worcestershire sauce, and 4 tablespoons of the butter in a medium saucepan and cook over medium-low heat until the butter melts.

INGREDIENTS

6½ tablespoons unsalted butter

1 cup panko bread crumbs

Salt and black pepper, to taste

1 medium zucchini, halved lengthwise
and cut into half-moons

1 red bell pepper, seeded and sliced

1 yellow bell pepper, seeded and sliced

3 tablespoons olive oil

2 medium carrots, thinly sliced
on the diagonal

1½ cups heavy cream

¼ teaspoon Worcestershire sauce

1½ cups Parmesan cheese,
grated, plus more for garnish

1 teaspoon nutmeg, grated

¾ pound pasta

2 handfuls of parsley, chopped,
for garnish

2 handfuls of basil, chopped,
for garnish

Gently stir in the Parmesan, season with salt and pepper, and add the nutmeg. Bring to a gentle simmer and cook until it thickens slightly, about 2 to 3 minutes. Remove from the heat, cover, and set aside.

4 Once the water is boiling, add salt (1 tablespoon of salt for every 4 cups water), stir, add the pasta, and cook 2 minutes short of the directed time. Reserve ¼ cup of pasta water, drain, and return the pot to the stove. Add reserved pasta water and the remaining butter, raise the heat to high, add the pasta, and cook until water is absorbed. Add the contents of the skillet and the roasted vegetables and cook, while gently tossing, for 2 minutes. Top with the toasted bread crumbs and garnish with the parsley, basil, and additional Parmesan before serving.

Alexia's Meat and Tortellini Skillet Dish

YIELD: 4 TO 6 SERVINGS • ACTIVE TIME: 20 MINUTES
TOTAL TIME: 50 MINUTES

If you or a loved one is in need of some comfort, break out this hearty preparation. The result is reminiscent of Hamburger Helper, though much fresher and tastier.

1 Place the peas in a colander and run warm water over them for 1 minute. Drain and set aside.

2 Heat a Dutch oven over medium-low heat for 2 to 3 minutes. Add the oil and raise the heat to medium-high. When the oil glistens, add the onion and a couple pinches of salt and stir. When the onion begins to sizzle, reduce the heat to low, cover, and cook, while stirring occasionally, until the onions are very soft, about 30 minutes.

3 Raise the heat to medium-high and add the ground meats. Season generously with salt, use a wooden spoon to break up the meat, and cook until the meat is a grayish brown, about 8 to 10 minutes.

4 Add the tomato paste and Worcestershire sauce, cook for 1 minute, and then add the broth and peas. Stir, bring to a boil, add the tortellini, and reduce the heat to medium. Cover and cook, while stirring occasionally, until the tortellini are tender but chewy, 3 to 4 minutes. Remove from heat, add the Parmesan, and stir well. Season with pepper and garnish with additional Parmesan before serving.

INGREDIENTS

1 (10 oz.) bag of frozen peas

2 tablespoons extra virgin olive oil

1 large yellow onion, minced

Salt and black pepper, to taste

½ pound ground beef

½ pound ground pork

2 tablespoons tomato paste

1½ teaspoons Worcestershire sauce

1¼ cups beef or chicken broth

1 (20 oz.) package of cheese tortellini

1 cup Parmesan cheese, grated, plus more for garnish

Asian Noodles

While Italy is what springs into the minds of many when they consider the origin of their favorite noodle, it is essential to recognize that it was the Chinese who opened the door for noodles to worm their way into everyone's hearts (and no, not via Marco Polo. Historical records show that pasta was being produced in Sicily a full century before he returned from his famous journey East). The Chinese spearheaded the charge in transforming wheat into dough, igniting the revolution that has transformed the cuisines all over the world. Since they did not have access to the durum wheat Italians used to produce their famed dried pasta, Asian countries traditionally utilized fresh dough to produce bouncy, springy noodles that were perfect for showcasing fresh ingredients. That tradition continues to this day, as you'll see in dishes like Chicken Lo Mein with Bean Sprouts, Cabbage, and Carrots (see pages 116–117) and Soba Noodles with Marinated Eggplant and Tofu (see pages 126–127).

Chicken Lo Mein with Bean Sprouts, Cabbage, and Carrots

YIELD: 4 TO 6 SERVINGS • ACTIVE TIME: 45 MINUTES
TOTAL TIME: 45 MINUTES

A dish found in any Chinese restaurant that's worth its weight in noodles, this lo mein is easy to put together and, quite frankly, will taste much better than what you can get almost anywhere.

1 Whisk the cornstarch, water, and the 2 teaspoons of peanut oil together in a medium bowl until combined. Add the chicken and toss until the chicken is evenly coated.

2 Bring a medium pot of water to a boil. Add the sprouts to the boiling water and cook for 2 minutes. Remove them with a strainer, immediately run them under cold water, and set aside.

3 Bring a large pot of water to a boil, add the noodles, and cook until tender but still chewy, 2 to 3 minutes. Drain and transfer to a medium bowl. Add ½ tablespoon of the peanut oil and toss. Set aside.

4 Heat a wok or large skillet over medium heat for 2 to 3 minutes. Add 2 tablespoons of the peanut oil and raise the heat to medium-high. When the oil glistens, add the chicken and cook until golden brown, about 2 to 3 minutes. Transfer to a warmed plate and cover loosely with aluminum foil to keep warm. Add the remaining peanut oil and the garlic, stir, and then add the cabbage, carrots, and a couple pinches of salt. Cook for 2 minutes, add the rice wine, stir, and then add the noodles and chicken. Cook, while tossing, for 1 minute. Cover and let steam for 1 minute.

5 Remove the lid, add the soy sauce, sesame oil, and sugar, and stir. Cook for 1 minute, add the bean sprouts and scallions, and cook, while stirring, for 1 minute.

INGREDIENTS

2 teaspoons cornstarch

2 teaspoons water

4½ tablespoons peanut oil, plus 2 teaspoons

½ pound boneless, skinless chicken breast, thinly sliced

2 cups mung bean sprouts, picked over

½ pound Chinese egg noodles, homemade (see pages 44–45) or store-bought

2 garlic cloves, minced

4 cups cabbage, shredded

2 medium carrots, julienned

Salt, to taste

1 tablespoon Shaoxing rice wine or dry sherry

2½ tablespoons dark soy sauce

1 teaspoon toasted sesame oil

½ teaspoon sugar

4 scallions, trimmed and thinly sliced

INGREDIENTS

½ pound pork loin or tenderloin, cubed

2 tablespoons Shaoxing rice wine, mirin, or dry sherry

1-inch piece of fresh ginger, peeled and grated

Salt, to taste

½ teaspoon black pepper

½ cup black bean paste

4 tablespoons grapeseed oil

2 tablespoons sugar

1½ pounds Chinese egg noodles, homemade (see pages 44–45) or store-bought

1 large onion, diced

1½ cups cabbage, roughly chopped

1 large zucchini, cubed

2 cups chicken or vegetable broth

2 tablespoons cornstarch, dissolved in ¼ cup water

1 small cucumber, peeled, seeded, and julienned

Chinese Egg Noodles with Pork and Black Bean Sauce

YIELD: 4 SERVINGS • ACTIVE TIME: 25 MINUTES
TOTAL TIME: 40 MINUTES

This sweet-and-savory dish is a subtle twist on jajangmyeon, a Korean dish that parents traditionally serve to celebrate their children's birthdays, exam days, and graduations. Pork is the classic option for this dish, but beef, chicken, and shrimp can all be substituted.

1 Combine the pork cubes, rice wine, ginger, a couple pinches of salt, and pepper in a medium bowl and mix well. Let marinate at room temperature for 15 minutes.

2 Place the black bean paste, 2 tablespoons of the oil, and the sugar in a small saucepan and cook over medium heat for 2 to 3 minutes, while stirring constantly, until it becomes a runny paste. Remove from heat and set aside.

3 Bring a large pot of water to a boil. Add the noodles and cook until they are tender but still chewy, about 2 to 3 minutes. Drain, rinse with warm water, and set aside.

4 Heat a wok or a large skillet over medium heat for 2 to 3 minutes. Turn the heat to medium-high, add the remaining oil, and let warm for 1 minute. Add the pork and cook until it begins to brown, about 3 to 4 minutes. Transfer to a warm bowl and cover loosely with aluminum foil.

5 Add the onion, cabbage, and zucchini to the pan, season with salt, and cook, while stirring occasionally, until the vegetables are soft, 5 to 6 minutes. Add the pork and the black bean paste mixture and toss until everything is well coated. Add the broth, bring to a boil, and cook for 3 to 4 minutes. Add the cornstarch, stir until combined, and cook until the sauce thickens, 1 to 2 minutes. Season to taste, divide the noodles between serving dishes, top with the contents of the pan, and garnish with the cucumber.

Fried Noodles

This version of a classic Malaysian dish substitutes crispy, chewy baby bok choy for the shrimp and squid. This leafy dark green vegetable is slightly bitter, similar to mustard greens, and has a light peppery flavor that brings out the strong, spicy flavor of this dish.

1 Add the bok choy, ¼ cup water, and a couple pinches of salt to a large skillet and cook over medium heat. When the water starts to boil, cover and let steam for 2 minutes. Remove from heat and set aside.

2 Bring a pot of water to boil and add the noodles. Cook until tender but chewy, about 2 to 3 minutes. Use tongs to transfer the noodles to a medium bowl, add ½ tablespoon of the oil, and toss. Keep the water in the pot boiling.

3 Add the sprouts to the boiling water and cook for 2 minutes. Remove them from the water with a strainer, immediately run under cold water, drain, and set aside.

4 Heat a wok or large skillet over medium heat for 2 to 3 minutes. Add the remaining oil, raise heat to medium-high, and then add the onion, cumin, coriander, and a pinch of salt. Cook for 1 minute. Add the green beans, tofu, and a pinch of salt, stir gently, and cook until the tofu turns a light golden brown, about 3 to 4 minutes. Add the bok choy, cook for 2 minutes, and then add the noodles. Cook, while tossing, until the noodles are warmed through. Add the soy sauces, the sambal oelek or Sriracha, and bean sprouts and cook, while stirring, for 1 minute. Serve with additional sambal oelek or Sriracha, lime wedges, lettuce, and chilies.

INGREDIENTS

6 baby bok choy, halved lengthwise

Salt, to taste

¾ pound Chinese egg noodles, homemade (see pages 44–45) or store-bought

2½ tablespoons peanut or grapeseed oil

½ cup mung bean sprouts, picked over

1 small onion, diced

1½ teaspoons ground cumin

1 teaspoon ground coriander

⅓ pound green beans, trimmed and halved

½ pound firm tofu, drained and cut into ½-inch strips

1 tablespoon dark soy sauce

1½ teaspoons light soy sauce

1½ teaspoons sambal oelek or Sriracha, plus more for serving

Lime wedges, for serving

Iceberg lettuce, thinly sliced, for serving

Thai bird chilies, thinly sliced, for serving

VARIATIONS:

- VEGETABLES SUCH AS SCALLIONS, CARROTS, MUSHROOMS, BROCCOLI, CHILI PEPPERS, BABY CORN
- GRILLED NY STRIP STEAK
- TERIYAKI-MARINATED CHICKEN

VARIATION: BEET GREENS WILL ALSO WORK WELL IN THIS DISH.

INGREDIENTS

½ teaspoon salt, plus more to taste

½ teaspoon cayenne paper, plus more to taste

½ teaspoon brown sugar

½ teaspoon chili powder

⅓ cup cashew butter

¼ cup soy sauce

1½ tablespoons rice vinegar

2½ teaspoons toasted sesame oil

2 teaspoons hot chili oil

¾ teaspoon sugar

2 garlic cloves, minced

3 tablespoons grapeseed oil

2 medium bone-in chicken breasts

¾ pound Chinese egg noodles, homemade (see pages 44-45) or store-bought

1 pound Swiss chard, stems discarded, sliced into ribbons

5 or 6 scallions, trimmed and thinly sliced

Egg Noodles with Chicken and Cashew Butter

YIELD: 4 SERVINGS • ACTIVE TIME: 40 MINUTES
TOTAL TIME: 45 MINUTES

The cashew butter lends a rich and creamy quality that brings the best out of both the Swiss chard and the spicy chicken.

1 Preheat the oven to 400°F. Place the salt, cayenne pepper, brown sugar, and chili powder in a small bowl and stir until well combined.

2 Place the cashew butter, soy sauce, rice vinegar, sesame oil, chili oil, sugar, and garlic in a medium bowl and stir until well combined.

3 Heat a large cast-iron skillet over medium heat for 2 to 3 minutes. Turn the heat to medium-high and add the grapeseed oil. Rub the spice mixture in the bowl over the chicken. When the oil glistens, add the chicken and cook, turning every 2 minutes, until nicely browned, about 6 to 8 minutes. Transfer the skillet to the oven and roast, turning the chicken over after 5 minutes, until the interior reaches 165°F, about 10 minutes. Remove skillet from the oven, transfer the breasts to a plate, and let cool. Once cool enough to handle, shred the chicken with your hands and set the meat aside.

4 While the chicken is roasting, bring a large pot of water to a boil. Once it's boiling, add salt (1 tablespoon for every 4 cups water), stir, add the noodles, and cook for 1 minute. Add the Swiss chard and cook until the noodles are still firm and chewy, about 1 to 2 minutes.

5 Drain and transfer to a large bowl. Add the shredded chicken and the cashew butter mixture, toss to coat evenly, and top with the scallions before serving.

Mongolian Beef with Crispy Chow Mein Noodles

**YIELD: 4 SERVINGS • ACTIVE TIME: 45 MINUTES
TOTAL TIME: ABOUT 4 HOURS**

This dish is a delightful combination of textures, with the crunchy noodles providing a lovely contrast to the tender and chewy fried beef.

INGREDIENTS

1 pound flank steak

1 (12 oz.) bottle of beer

1 tablespoon toasted sesame oil

3 garlic cloves, thinly sliced

2-inch piece of fresh ginger, peeled and grated

½ cup soy sauce

½ cup water

1½ tablespoons molasses

1 teaspoon Sriracha, plus more to taste

⅔ cup brown sugar, firmly packed

¾ pound Chinese egg noodles, homemade (see pages 44–45) or store-bought

2 cups grapeseed oil, plus 4 tablespoons

2 tablespoons cornstarch

8 baby bok choy, quartered lengthwise, and blanched

Salt, to taste

1 Put the flank steak and beer in a large resealable plastic bag. Place in a shallow pan and marinate in the refrigerator for 3 hours, turning the bag over a few times. Let the steak come to room temperature before cooking.

2 Heat a small saucepan over medium heat for 1 minute. Add the sesame oil, heat for 1 minute, then add the garlic and ginger and cook until fragrant, about 1 minute. Add the soy sauce and the water and bring to a boil. Add the molasses, Sriracha, and brown sugar and cook, while stirring frequently, until the sauce thickens, about 5 minutes. Remove from heat and set aside.

3 Bring a large pot of water to a boil and add the noodles. Cook for 2 to 3 minutes, until they are tender but chewy. Drain and place them on a kitchen towel to dry.

4 Working in two batches, heat a medium skillet over low heat for 2 to 3 minutes. Add 2 tablespoons of the grapeseed oil and raise the heat to medium-high. When the oil is glistening, add half of the noodles and cook without touching them for 3 to 4 minutes, until they are golden brown and crispy. Carefully flip the cake of noodles over and cook for 3 minutes. Transfer to a paper towel-lined plate to dry, add 2 more tablespoons of the oil, and repeat with the remaining noodles.

5 Slice the steak into thin strips, cutting against the grain. Place the strips in a medium bowl with the cornstarch and toss until evenly coated. Heat a deep saucepan over low heat for 2 minutes. Add the remaining oil, raise the heat to medium-high, and heat the oil until it reaches 360°F. Add 4 slices of steak, cook for 1½ minutes, remove with a slotted spoon, and transfer to a paper towel-lined platter. Cover with aluminum foil and repeat with the remaining slices of steak.

6 Transfer the cooked steak to a medium bowl, add ¾ cup of the sauce, and toss. Cut the crispy noodle cakes in half and place them on four plates. Top with the steak slices and bok choy and serve with the remaining sauce.

Soba Noodles with Marinated Eggplant and Tofu

YIELD: 4 SERVINGS • ACTIVE TIME: 45 MINUTES
TOTAL TIME: 2 HOURS

The chewy noodles and crispy tofu make a satisfying backdrop for the lightly caramelized eggplant and tangy ginger-soy dressing.

1 Combine all the marinade ingredients in a small bowl. Combine all the dressing ingredients in another small bowl. Set both aside.

2 Place the pieces of eggplant in a medium bowl and toss with the marinade. Let stand for 1 hour at room temperature. Drain the tofu and cut it into ½-inch strips. Arrange them in a single layer on a paper-towel lined tray. Cover with paper towels and pat dry. Let them sit for 30 minutes, changing the paper towels after 15 minutes. Cut the strips into ½-inch cubes.

3 Bring a large pot of water to boil. When it's boiling, add the noodles and cook until they are tender but chewy, 5 to 7 minutes. Drain, rinse under cold water, drain again, and place in a large bowl. Toss with the dressing and set aside.

4 Heat a wok or large skillet over medium heat for 2 to 3 minutes. Raise the heat to medium-high and add 2 tablespoons of the peanut oil. When it begins to glisten, add the eggplant cubes and a couple pinches of salt and stir-fry until they soften and turn golden, 5 to 6 minutes. Using a slotted spoon, transfer the eggplant to a paper towel-lined plate. Add the remaining peanut oil to the wok and add the tofu cubes. Stir-fry until they turn golden all over, 4 to 5 minutes. Transfer them to another paper towel-lined plate. Divide the soba noodles among four bowls, top with the eggplant and tofu, and garnish with the scallions.

INGREDIENTS

For the Marinade

2 tablespoons rice vinegar

3 tablespoons soy sauce

1 tablespoon toasted sesame oil

½ teaspoon sugar

2 garlic cloves, minced

For the Dressing

1 tablespoon rice vinegar

1 tablespoon peanut oil

1 teaspoon soy sauce

1 tablespoon toasted sesame oil

1-inch piece of ginger, peeled and grated

For the Eggplants & Tofu

3 Chinese eggplants (about 2 pounds), ends trimmed and cubed

¾ pound firm tofu

½ pound soba noodles

3 tablespoons peanut oil

Salt, to taste

5 scallions, trimmed and sliced into ¼-inch pieces, for garnish

Soba Noodle Stir-Fry

YIELD: 4 SERVINGS • ACTIVE TIME: 20 MINUTES
TOTAL TIME: 30 MINUTES

You don't need a side salad with this savory soba noodle dish. Of course, this versatile stir-fry is just as satisfying with Chinese egg noodles and rice noodles, but soba's nutty flavor lends an additional welcomed dimension to the savory vegetables.

1 Combine the soy sauce, water, rice vinegar, and 2 teaspoons of the sesame oil in a bowl and set aside. Bring a large pot of water to a boil. When it's boiling, add the noodles and cook until they are tender but chewy, 5 to 7 minutes. Drain, rinse under cold water, drain again, and place in a large bowl. Toss with the remaining sesame oil to keep them from sticking.

2 Heat a wok or a large skillet over medium heat for 2 to 3 minutes. Turn the heat to medium-high and add the grapeseed oil. When it begins to glisten, add the onion, carrots, asparagus, mushrooms, chard, and salt. Stir-fry until the vegetables are tender, 4 to 5 minutes. Lower the heat to medium, add the garlic and stir-fry until fragrant, about 1 minute. Add the soba noodles and edamame and continue to toss until heated through. Add the soy sauce-and-rice vinegar mixture and toss well. Divide the noodles and vegetables among four warm plates and serve immediately.

INGREDIENTS

¼ cup soy sauce

3 tablespoons water

1½ tablespoons rice vinegar

3 teaspoons toasted sesame oil

½ pound soba noodles

3 tablespoons grapeseed oil

1 yellow onion, thinly sliced

2 carrots, peeled and julienned

1 pound asparagus, ends trimmed, sliced into ¼-inch pieces

6 shiitake mushrooms, stemmed and chopped

1 pound Swiss chard, stemmed and chopped

1 teaspoon salt

2 garlic cloves, minced

⅓ cup edamame, shelled and cooked

INGREDIENTS

1 pound rice stick noodles

2½ tablespoons toasted sesame oil

2 tablespoons tahini

1½ tablespoons smooth peanut butter

¼ cup soy sauce

2 tablespoons rice vinegar

1 tablespoon light brown sugar

2 teaspoons chili-garlic sauce, plus more for serving (optional)

2-inch piece of fresh ginger, peeled and grated

2 garlic cloves, minced

1 yellow or orange bell pepper, seeded and thinly sliced

1 cucumber, peeled, seeded, and thinly sliced

1 cup snow peas, trimmed

½ cup roasted peanuts, chopped, for garnish

2 tablespoons sesame seeds, toasted, for garnish

5 or 6 scallions, white and light green parts only, sliced into ½-inch pieces, for garnish

Garden Sesame Noodles

Few Chinese dishes are as synonymous with take-out as sesame noodles, but the irony is that they are so easy to prepare and so much more delicious when homemade. This is the perfect dinner when you just want something light before curling up on the couch.

1 Bring a large pot of water to a boil. Add the noodles and cook until tender but still chewy, 2 to 3 minutes. Drain and transfer the noodles to a large bowl. Add ½ tablespoon of the sesame oil and toss to prevent them from sticking together.

2 Place the tahini and the peanut butter in a small bowl. Add the soy sauce, vinegar, remaining sesame oil, brown sugar, chili-garlic sauce (if using), ginger, and garlic and whisk together until smooth. Taste for seasoning and adjust the flavors according to your preference.

3 Add the sauce to the noodles and toss until well distributed. Arrange the noodles in six bowls and top with the pepper slivers, cucumber slices, and snow peas. Garnish with the peanuts, sesame seeds, and scallions and serve with additional chili-garlic sauce, if desired.

Singapore Rice Noodles with Shrimp and Curry

**YIELD: 8 SERVINGS • ACTIVE TIME: 50 MINUTES
TOTAL TIME: 1 HOUR AND 15 MINUTES**

This dish contains curry powder, but not just any curry powder—the gorgeously colored and full-bodied Maharajah, which is comprised of prized spices such as saffron, cumin, ginger, and nutmeg.

1 Soak the noodles in a medium bowl of warm water until softened, about 20 minutes. Drain well, wipe the bowl with a paper towel, and return the noodles to it. Toss with ½ tablespoon of the peanut oil to prevent them from sticking together.

2 Heat a wok or large skillet over medium heat for 2 to 3 minutes. Turn the heat to medium-high and add 1 tablespoon of the peanut oil. When it begins to glisten, add the eggs and 2 pinches of salt and cook until set, 2 to 3 minutes. Transfer to a plate until cool, and then slice into thin, 2-inch-long slivers.

3 Add the sesame oil to the pan. Blot the pork with paper towels to remove as much surface moisture as possible. Once the oil begins to glisten, sprinkle the pork with salt, add it to the pan, and reduce the heat to medium. Cook, while turning occasionally, until completely cooked, 6 to 10 minutes. Transfer it to a cutting board. When it's cool enough to handle, cut it into ¼-inch-thick strips that are 1 inch long.

4 Pat the shrimp dry with paper towels. Heat the pan and add 1 tablespoon of the peanut oil. When the surface of the oil

INGREDIENTS

2 (6 to 8 oz. each) packages of rice stick noodles

8½ tablespoons peanut oil

5 large eggs, lightly beaten

Salt, to taste

2 tablespoons toasted sesame oil

1 pound pork tenderloin

1 pound shrimp, peeled, deveined, and tails removed

1 yellow onion, cut into half-moons

2 jalapeño peppers, seeded and minced

2-inch piece of ginger, peeled and grated

6 black garlic cloves, minced

2 red bell peppers, seeded and thinly sliced

½ cup green cabbage, thinly sliced

½ pound cremini mushrooms, stemmed and thinly sliced

5 scallions, white and light green parts only, cut into 1½-inch pieces

6 oz. snow peas, trimmed

½ teaspoon freshly ground white pepper

½ teaspoon ground coriander

½ teaspoon sesame seeds, toasted

¼ cup Maharajah curry powder

1 cup chicken broth

begins to glisten, raise the heat to medium-high, add the shrimp and a couple pinches of salt, and stir-fry until the shrimp are firm and cooked through, 4 to 5 minutes. Transfer to the cutting board with the pork.

5 Add 2 tablespoons of the peanut oil to the pan. When it glistens, add the onion, jalapeños, ginger, and garlic and cook until the onion is translucent, 6 to 7 minutes. Add the peppers, cabbage, mushrooms, scallions, snow peas, white pepper, coriander, toasted sesame seeds, and a pinch of salt and stir-fry for 1 minute. Place the curry, broth, and the remaining peanut oil in a small bowl and stir to combine. Pour over the vegetables in the pan and let simmer for 3 to 4 minutes. Add the pork, shrimp, eggs, and rice stick noodles and toss until coated. Season to taste and serve immediately.

Vietnamese Noodle Salad

YIELD: 4 SERVINGS • ACTIVE TIME: 30 MINUTES
TOTAL TIME: 50 MINUTES

Vietnamese cuisine excels at contrasting flavors and textures, and this "noodle salad" is no exception. Complete with chewy noodles, crunchy bean sprouts and peanuts, soft tofu, and a salty sweet-and-sour sauce, it is complex flavorwise yet incredibly simple to prepare.

INGREDIENTS

For the Salad

1 pound extra-firm tofu, drained and cut into ½-inch strips

2 cups mung bean sprouts, picked over

½ pound dotori guksu (Korean acorn noodles) or dried rice stick noodles

¼ cup peanut oil

Salt, to taste

2½ cups romaine lettuce, shredded

2 handfuls of mixed fresh herbs, coarsely chopped (mint, cilantro, basil)

2 small cucumbers, peeled and julienned

2 tablespoons salted, roasted peanuts, chopped, for garnish

For the Nuoc Cham

⅓ cup hot water

¼ cup fresh lime juice

¼ cup fish sauce

¼ cup brown sugar

3 tablespoons rice vinegar

3 garlic cloves, minced

1-inch piece of fresh ginger, peeled and grated

1 jalapeño pepper, seeded and chopped

1 Place the tofu in a single layer on a paper towel-lined tray. Cover with paper towels and pat dry. Let them sit for 30 minutes, changing the paper towels after 15 minutes. Cut the dried strips into ½-inch cubes and set aside.

2 Bring a large pot of water to a boil. Place the bean sprouts in a bowl of cold water and discard the hulls that float to the top. Rinse under cold water, add to the boiling water, and cook for 1 minute. Remove them from the water with a strainer and run under cold water. Drain well and chop. Add the noodles to the pot of boiling water and cook until they are tender but chewy, 5 to 7 minutes. Drain, rinse under cold water, and drain again.

3 Prepare the Nuoc Cham. Combine all of the ingredients in a small bowl and stir until the sugar dissolves. This can be prepared up to 3 to 4 hours in advance and refrigerated; bring back to room temperature before using.

4 Heat a large, deep skillet over medium heat for 2 to 3 minutes. Add the peanut oil, raise the heat to medium-high, and let it warm up for 1 or 2 minutes. Sprinkle the tofu with salt. When the surface of the oil begins to glisten, add the tofu in a single layer (you may need to work in two batches). Cook until golden on all sides, 4 to 6 minutes total. Transfer to a paper towel-lined plate to drain.

5 Divide the noodles between four shallow bowls. Arrange the lettuce, herbs, cucumber, and tofu on top. Drizzle with the Nuoc Cham and garnish with the peanuts.

Spicy Cellophane Noodles with Green Beans and Tofu

**YIELD: 4 SERVINGS • ACTIVE TIME: 40 MINUTES
TOTAL TIME: 1 HOUR**

Cellophane noodles are used to good effect in this spicy vegetarian stir-fry. Fresh green beans are also key, so make sure you load up when they're bountiful and inexpensive at the farmers market.

1 Place the tofu in a single layer on a paper towel-lined tray. Cover with paper towels and pat dry. Let them sit for 30 minutes, changing the paper towels after 15 minutes. Cut the dried pieces into strips and set aside.

2 Place the noodles in a large bowl and cover with 2 quarts of hot water. Let sit until the noodles become soft and pliable, about 15 minutes. Rinse with cold water and drain well. Heat a wok or large skillet over medium heat for 2 to 3 minutes. Turn the heat to medium-high and add 2 tablespoons of the oil. When it begins to glisten, add ½ of the tofu and cook until crispy and brown on all sides. Carefully transfer to a paper towel-lined plate. Repeat with the remaining tofu and peanut oil.

3 Add the shallots and a couple pinches of salt to the pan and cook until tender and golden brown, 3 to 4 minutes. Add the garlic, red pepper flakes, and green beans and stir-fry until the beans are tender and bright green, 3 to 4 minutes. Add the tofu and brown sugar and cook until the tofu is heated through, about 3 minutes. Add the noodles, soy sauce, and fish sauce, and toss together until heated through, 2 to 3 minutes. Remove from the heat and toss with the lime juice and half of the Thai basil. Divide among four warm shallow bowls and garnish with peanuts and the remaining Thai basil.

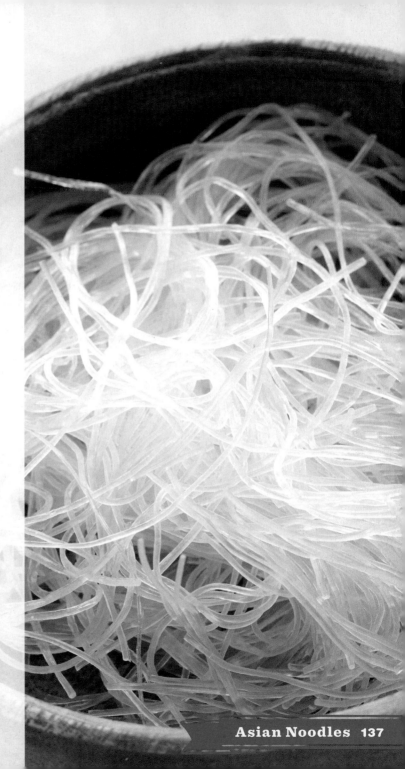

INGREDIENTS

10 oz. extra-firm tofu, drained and cut into ¾-inch pieces

½ pound dry cellophane noodles

4 tablespoons peanut oil, plus more as needed

3 large shallots, minced

Salt, to taste

2 garlic cloves, minced

1 teaspoon red pepper flakes

1 pound green beans, trimmed and cut into 2-inch pieces

2 tablespoons light brown sugar

2 tablespoons soy sauce

2 tablespoons fish sauce

Juice of 2 limes

½ cup Thai basil, chopped

⅓ cup roasted peanuts, coarsely chopped

Ants Climbing a Tree

The unusual name comes from an imaginative estimation that the noodles, chopped scallions, and ground meat resemble, respectively, tree branches, green leaves, and ants.

INGREDIENTS

- ½ pound cellophane noodles
- 2½ tablespoons peanut oil
- 4 oz. ground pork
- 4 oz. ground beef
- 1½ tablespoons light soy sauce
- ⅛ teaspoon salt
- 1½ tablespoons chili bean paste
- 1 teaspoon dark soy sauce
- ¾ cup hot chicken broth
- 3 scallions, white and light green parts only, thinly sliced

1 Soak the noodles in a medium bowl of warm water until softened, about 20 minutes. Drain well, wipe the bowl with a paper towel, and return the noodles to it. Toss with ½ tablespoon of the oil to prevent them from sticking together.

2 Combine the pork, beef, ½ tablespoon of the light soy sauce, and the salt in another medium bowl and stir until well combined. Heat a wok or large skillet over medium heat for 2 to 3 minutes. Raise the heat to high and add the remaining oil. When it begins to glisten, add the ground meat mixture and cook, while stirring and pressing down on it often, until it begins to brown, 5 to 7 minutes. Add the chili bean paste and the dark soy sauce and stir until well combined. Add the noodles, remaining light soy sauce, and broth and toss to thoroughly coat the noodles. Reduce the heat to medium-low, cover, and simmer until there is very little moisture in the pan, 8 to 10 minutes. Carefully shake the pan, sprinkle the scallions over the top, and serve immediately.

Rice Noodles with Beef and Broccoli

YIELD: 4 SERVINGS • ACTIVE TIME: 30 MINUTES
TOTAL TIME: 45 MINUTES

A wonderful meal to add to your weeknight repertoire. If you can find it, Chinese broccoli, which looks like elongated Swiss chard but actually tastes like bolder and slightly more bitter broccoli, takes this dish to another level.

1 Place the baking soda, the soy sauce, and the pepper in a medium bowl and whisk to combine. Add the steak slices and toss until they are evenly coated. Cover and set aside.

2 Trim each stalk of broccoli about 1½ inches from the bottom. Keep the stalks and leafy parts separate as you prep them. Cut the stalks into approximately ½-inch-thick slices and chop the green leafy sections into 2-inch pieces. If using regular broccoli, cut the stems in the same way and the florets into bite-sized pieces.

3 Combine 6 tablespoons of the broth and the cornstarch in a medium bowl and whisk until smooth. Whisk in the oyster sauce and soybean paste (or red miso paste), then gradually whisk in the rest of the broth. Set the mixture aside.

4 Bring a large pot of water to a boil and add the noodles. Cook according to the manufacturer's instructions until they are tender but chewy. Drain, rinse under cold water, drain again, and place them on a kitchen towel to dry.

5 Place a skillet over high heat, add the oil and the garlic, and stir-fry for about

INGREDIENTS

2 teaspoons baking soda

3 tablespoons soy sauce

¾ teaspoon black pepper

1 pound rib-eye steak, thinly sliced against the grain

1¾ pounds broccoli, Chinese or standard

6 cups chicken broth

6 tablespoons cornstarch

2 tablespoons oyster sauce

2 teaspoons fermented soybean paste or red miso paste

¾ pound wide rice noodles

2 tablespoons peanut oil

6 garlic cloves, minced

¼ cup sesame seeds, for garnish

30 seconds. Add the beef and broccoli stalks and cook, while stirring frequently, until the meat is almost cooked through, about 2 to 3 minutes. Add the remaining broccoli and cook for an additional minute. Pour the chicken broth mixture over the ingredients and cook, stirring occasionally, until the sauce thickens, about 2 minutes. Divide the noodles between the bowls, top with the mixture in the skillet, and garnish with the sesame seeds.

Shrimp and Tofu Pad Thai

YIELD: 4 SERVINGS • ACTIVE TIME: 45 MINUTES
TOTAL TIME: 1 HOUR AND 15 MINUTES

Aficionados insist that the key to a truly spectacular pad thai lies in cooking its stretchy, chewy white noodles, called sen lek, to firm yet tender perfection; however, if sen lek noodles prove difficult to find, use flat rice noodles.

INGREDIENTS

½ pound extra-firm tofu,
drained and cut into ½-inch strips

1 cup mung bean sprouts, picked over

½ pound sen lek rice noodles

2½ tablespoons peanut oil

2 garlic cloves, minced

2 Thai chilies, very thinly sliced

⅓ cup light brown sugar, firmly packed

½ cup tamarind paste,
pureed with 1 tablespoon water

5 tablespoons fish sauce

Juice of ½ lime

1 pound large shrimp,
peeled and deveined

Salt, to taste

⅛ teaspoon red pepper flakes

3 large eggs, lightly beaten

2 scallions, white parts only, thinly sliced

2 carrots, peeled and julienned

Cilantro, chopped, for garnish

Roasted peanuts, chopped, for garnish

Lime wedges, for serving

1 Place the tofu in a single layer on a paper towel-lined tray. Cover with paper towels and pat dry. Let them sit for 30 minutes, changing the paper towels after 15 minutes. Cut the dried strips into matchsticks and set aside.

2 While the tofu drains, bring a medium saucepan of water to a boil. While it comes to a boil, place the bean sprouts in a bowl of cold water. Discard the hulls that float to the top. Rinse the remaining sprouts under cold water, add the sprouts to the boiling water, and cook for 2 minutes. Remove them with a strainer and immediately run under cold water. Drain well and chop.

3 Soak the noodles in a bowl of room temperature water until tender and chewy. Soaking time varies depending on the width of the noodles. (For ⅙-inch wide noodles, 20 to 25 minutes should be sufficient, but always taste test.) Drain, transfer to a medium bowl, and toss with ½ tablespoon of the oil to prevent any sticking.

4 Combine the garlic, chilies, sugar, tamarind paste, and fish sauce in a small saucepan. Raise the heat to medium and cook, while stirring, until the sugar and paste have dissolved, 2 to 3 minutes. Remove from heat and stir in the lime juice.

5 Heat a wok or large skillet over medium heat for 2 to 3 minutes. Once it is very hot, add the remaining oil and then add the shrimp, a couple pinches of salt, and the red pepper flakes and stir-fry until the shrimp begin to turn opaque and pink, about 3 minutes. Add the eggs and cook until just set, about 30 seconds. Use a rubber spatula to scramble the eggs and the shrimp. Add ⅓ of the garlic-chili mixture and the noodles and toss to combine. Add the tofu, bean sprouts, scallions, and carrots, toss, and cook until heated through, about 2 to 3 minutes. Garnish with the cilantro and peanuts and serve immediately with lime wedges.

Ramen Noodles and Tofu San Bei

YIELD: 4 SERVINGS • ACTIVE TIME: 30 MINUTES
TOTAL TIME: 1 HOUR

San bei, or "three cups," refers to the equal amounts of sesame oil, soy sauce, and rice wine traditionally used to make the extremely aromatic sauce for this Taiwanese dish. This recipe veers off the original path, varying these ratios and exchanging chicken and rice for tofu and ramen noodles.

1 Place the tofu in a single layer on a paper towel-lined tray. Cover with paper towels and pat dry. Let them sit for 30 minutes, changing the paper towels after 15 minutes. Set the dried strips aside.

2 Heat the largest skillet you have over medium heat for 2 to 3 minutes. Add the peanut oil and heat until it starts to glisten. Dredge the tofu slices in a shallow bowl filled with cornstarch and tap to remove any excess. Place the tofu in the skillet in a single layer (you will likely have to work in batches). Raise the heat to medium-high and cook until they are a golden caramel color, 3 to 4 minutes per side. Transfer to a paper towel-lined plate to drain.

3 Wipe out the skillet, add the sesame oil, and reduce the heat to medium. When the oil glistens, add the garlic, ginger, scallions, and two pinches of salt and cook, while stirring occasionally, until fragrant, about 2 minutes. Add the sugar, stir until it dissolves, and then add the ¾ cup of water, the wine or sherry, and the soy sauce. Increase the heat to medium-high and bring to a boil. Reduce the heat to low, cover, and simmer, while stirring occasionally, for 10 minutes.

4 Combine the remaining cornstarch and water in a small bowl, add the mixture to the skillet, and stir until well combined. Continue to cook, while stirring occasionally, until the sauce thickens, about 5 minutes. Add the tofu slices and cook until warmed through.

5 As the sauce simmers, bring a large pot of water to a boil. Add the ramen noodles and cook until tender and chewy. Drain, divide between warm bowls, top with the contents of the skillet, and garnish with the basil.

INGREDIENTS

1 pound extra-firm tofu, drained and cut into ½-inch slices

3 tablespoons peanut oil

1½ teaspoons cornstarch, plus more for dredging

3 tablespoons toasted sesame oil

8 garlic cloves, peeled and smashed

2-inch piece of ginger, peeled and sliced into 8 pieces

10 scallions, white parts only, cut into ½-inch pieces

Salt, to taste

3 tablespoons sugar

¾ cup water, plus 1 tablespoon

¾ cup Shaoxing rice wine or dry sherry

⅓ cup soy sauce

⅓ pound ramen noodles

2 handfuls of Thai basil leaves, thinly sliced, for garnish

Korean Noodles with Gochujang Sauce

**YIELD: 4 SERVINGS • ACTIVE TIME: 30 MINUTES
TOTAL TIME: 50 MINUTES**

This recipe features the unique and popular jjolmyeon noodles. The noodles' elastic chewiness complements the gochujang in the sweet and savory sauce. Gochujang is a thick, sticky, hot red chili paste that adds a spicy and very concentrated flavor to the sauce.

1 Combine the rice vinegar, water, sugar, gochujang, red pepper flakes, sesame oil, sesame seeds, garlic, and salt in a medium bowl and whisk until combined. Set the sauce aside.

2 Bring a large pot of water to a boil. While it is coming to a boil, place the bean sprouts in a bowl of cold water. Discard the hulls that float to the top. Rinse the remaining sprouts under cold water, add the sprouts to the boiling water, and cook for 1 minute. Remove them with a strainer and immediately run under cold water. Drain well and set aside. Place the noodles in the boiling water and cook until tender but chewy, 3 to 5 minutes. Drain, rub to remove excess starch as you rinse them under cold water, and then drain completely.

3 Divide the noodles between the serving bowls and then artfully arrange the sprouts, cabbage slivers, cucumber, carrots, and a piece of egg on top of each. Drizzle with the sauce and serve.

INGREDIENTS

6 tablespoons rice vinegar

5 tablespoons water

¼ cup sugar

3 tablespoons gochujang

2 tablespoons red pepper flakes

2 tablespoons toasted sesame oil

2 tablespoons sesame seeds, toasted

3 garlic cloves, peeled and minced

2 teaspoons salt, plus more to taste

2 cups mung bean sprouts, picked over

1½ pounds frozen jjolmyeon noodles, separated under cold running water

½ pound cabbage, thinly sliced

1 large cucumber, peeled and julienned

2 carrots, peeled and julienned

2 large hard-boiled eggs, halved lengthwise

Soups

Noodles and soup are two places to turn when we're in need of comfort. So it should come as no surprise that combining them provides unprecedented flavor and warmth. This chapter is brimming with simple standards from around the world, providing you with a host of solutions if you're seeking shelter from harsh weather or trying to cobble a meal together from the odds and ends in your pantry.

Whether it's a bowl of Pho (see pages 150–151), the Vietnamese classic, or Penicillin Soup with Egg Noodles (see pages 170–171), we're certain these noodle-based soups will provide a refuge from whatever the world's cooked up for you.

Pho

YIELD: 8 SERVINGS • ACTIVE TIME: 1 HOUR
TOTAL TIME: 5½ HOURS

This classic soup is served in Vietnam at any time of the day, even breakfast. The key to top-notch pho is a deeply flavored and intoxicatingly aromatic broth, so make sure to take your time with this one.

INGREDIENTS

2 small onions, halved

2-inch piece of fresh ginger, halved lengthwise

4 pounds beef shin bones, some meat attached

1 pound boneless beef chuck roast

8 whole cloves

6 star anise

1 cinnamon stick

2 teaspoons fennel seeds

5 scallions, trimmed and cut into 4-inch lengths

¼ cup fish sauce

2½ tablespoons sugar

1 tablespoon salt

¾ pound dried rice noodles

Cilantro, chopped, for garnish

Thai basil, chopped, for garnish

Thai chilies, thinly sliced, for garnish

Scallion greens, chopped, for garnish

Mung bean sprouts, picked over, for garnish

Lime wedges, for garnish

1 Preheat the broiler on your oven. Place the onions and ginger on a parchment-lined baking sheet and broil until lightly blackened on all sides, turning the pieces every 30 seconds or so for even cooking; it should take about 3 minutes all together. Remove from the oven and let cool. When cool enough to handle, remove and discard the charred skin.

2 Place the bones and chuck in a large pot and add water to cover. Bring to a boil and cook for 20 minutes. Drain and thoroughly wash the pot. Once the meat and bones are cool enough to handle, rinse them under cold water, wiping away any debris.

3 While the beef is cooling, place the cloves, star anise, cinnamon stick, and fennel seeds in a small skillet over medium-low heat and toast until fragrant, 3 to 4 minutes, shaking the pan several times. Transfer them to a piece of cheesecloth and tie into a bundle.

4 Add 4 quarts fresh water to the pot and bring to a boil. Add the meat and bones, onions, ginger, toasted spice sachet, scallions, fish sauce, sugar, and salt and stir. Bring to a boil over high heat, reduce the heat to low, and simmer for 1½ hours, skimming the surface as needed. Remove the piece of beef chuck to a small plate, tent with aluminum foil, and set aside. Once cooled, you can refrigerate until ready to use. Continue to simmer the stock for at least another 3 hours, skimming any fat and foam as necessary. It should have a deep, highly spiced flavor; in fact, it should taste so good that you would happily drink it. Strain through a fine sieve and discard the solids. Taste again and adjust seasoning, if necessary, by adding salt, sugar, and/or fish sauce.

5 While the stock simmers, prepare the noodles by soaking them in a bowl of room temperature water until they are pleasantly chewy, 20 to 30 minutes. Drain the noodles, rinse, cover, and refrigerate until ready to use.

6 Divide the noodles between the serving bowls. Cut the beef chuck into thin slices and divide the slices between the bowls. Bring the stock to a rolling boil, ladle it into the serving bowls, and serve alongside bowls containing the fresh herbs, chilies, scallions, bean sprouts, and lime wedges so everyone can tailor his or her soup to taste.

Sweet and Sour Egg Drop Soup

YIELD: 6 SERVINGS • ACTIVE TIME: 30 MINUTES
TOTAL TIME: 50 MINUTES

This tasty and nourishing soup may as well be prescribed. It combines the healing properties of chicken broth, the antiseptic qualities of vinegar, and the circulation-enhancing power of hot chili oil.

1 Place the tofu in a single layer on a paper towel-lined tray. Cover with paper towels and pat dry. Let them sit for 30 minutes, changing the paper towels after 15 minutes. Cut the dried strips into cubes and set aside.

2 While the tofu drains, bring a large pot of water to a boil and then add the noodles. Cook until tender but still chewy, drain, and rinse under cold water. Drain again, transfer to a medium bowl, and toss with ½ tablespoon of the sesame oil to prevent them from sticking.

3 Heat a Dutch oven over low heat for 2 to 3 minutes. Add 1 tablespoon of sesame oil and raise the heat to medium. When the oil begins to glisten, add the garlic, ginger, scallions, and a pinch of salt and cook, while stirring occasionally, for about 5 minutes. Add the pork and break up any large pieces with a wooden spoon. Cook, while stirring occasionally, until the meat is no longer pink, 8 to 10 minutes. Add the broth and bring to a gentle boil. Add the tofu, mushrooms, vinegar, soy sauce, sugar, the remaining sesame oil, and, if desired, the chili oil. Return to a gentle boil, reduce the heat to a simmer, taste the soup, and adjust the seasoning to taste.

4 Slowly whisk the eggs into the soup so that they form strands and bring the soup back to a simmer. Divide the noodles between six warm bowls and ladle the soup over them. Garnish with the scallion greens and toasted sesame seeds.

INGREDIENTS

1 pound extra-firm tofu, drained and cubed

10 oz. black rice ramen noodles

2½ tablespoons toasted sesame oil

3 garlic cloves, peeled and minced

2-inch piece of ginger, peeled and grated

6 scallions, white and light green parts only, thinly sliced, greens reserved for garnish

Salt, to taste

½ pound ground pork

8 cups chicken broth

8 cremini mushrooms, sliced

¼ cup rice vinegar

3 tablespoons soy sauce

2 teaspoons sugar

1 tablespoon hot chili oil (optional)

2 large eggs, beaten

Sesame seeds, toasted, for garnish

Miso Soup with Udon Noodles

**YIELD: 4 SERVINGS • ACTIVE TIME: 20 MINUTES
TOTAL TIME: 35 MINUTES**

Red miso, which contains soybeans, barley, and other grains, is the key to this dish. It is fermented longer than other miso pastes, yielding the rich, deep umami flavors that you can never have enough of.

1 Bring a large pot of water to a boil. When it's boiling, add the noodles and cook until tender but still chewy, about 2 minutes. Drain and divide the noodles between four warmed soup bowls.

2 While the water is coming to a boil, combine the broth, sake or wine, and ginger in a medium saucepan and bring to a boil over medium-high heat. Reduce the heat to medium-low and simmer for 5 minutes to let the flavors infuse. Remove the ginger with a slotted spoon and discard. Add the mushrooms and

carrot and simmer until the carrot just starts to soften, 4 to 5 minutes.

3 Place the miso in a small bowl and add ¼ cup of the hot broth. Stir until the miso dissolves and the liquid looks creamy, then pour it into the broth.

4 Warm up the tofu by placing it in a sieve and running a slow stream of hot tap water over it for 1 minute. Divide the tofu between the serving bowls and ladle the hot broth into them. Garnish with the scallions.

INGREDIENTS

¾ pound udon
noodles, homemade
(see pages 46–47)
or store-bought

6 cups chicken or
vegetable broth

3 tablespoons sake
or rice wine

2-inch piece of ginger,
peeled and
thinly sliced

4 cremini mushrooms,
trimmed and
thinly sliced

1 carrot, very thinly
sliced

1½ tablespoons
red miso paste

4 oz. silken tofu,
drained and cut into
½-inch cubes

5 scallions, dark
green parts only,
thinly sliced, for
garnish

INGREDIENTS

8 cups chicken broth

3 star anise

2 cinnamon sticks

8 shiitake mushrooms, stemmed and chopped

4 baby bok choy, cut into bite-sized pieces

1 pound udon noodles, homemade (see pages 46–47) or store-bought

6 tablespoons soy sauce

5 scallions, white and light green parts only, thinly sliced

2 hard-boiled eggs, halved

2 red chilies, thinly sliced, for garnish

Black sesame seeds, for garnish

Udon Noodle Soup with Baby Bok Choy and Eggs

**YIELD: 4 SERVINGS • ACTIVE TIME: 10 MINUTES
TOTAL TIME: 25 MINUTES**

Udon noodles lend their irresistible chewiness to this simple yet aromatic soup that is brimming with the earthy flavor of shiitake mushrooms and the warmth of cinnamon.

1 Bring the broth to a simmer in a large pot over medium-high heat. Add the star anise and cinnamon sticks, reduce the heat to low, and simmer for 10 minutes. Remove the star anise and cinnamon stick with a slotted spoon and discard.

2 Add the mushrooms to the simmering broth and stir. Add the bok choy, gently pushing down to submerge them in the broth. Cook for about 3 minutes.

3 While the broth is simmering, bring a large pot of water to a boil, add the noodles, and cook until tender but still chewy, about 2 minutes. Drain and divide the noodles between four warmed soup bowls. Remove the large pot from the stove and add the soy sauce and scallions. Stir gently, season to taste, and divide the soup between the serving bowls, making sure each gets a piece of egg and an even amount of the bok choy. Garnish with the chilies and black sesame seeds and serve.

Korean Cold Noodle Soup

**YIELD: 4 SERVINGS • ACTIVE TIME: 35 MINUTES
TOTAL TIME: 3 HOURS**

Koreans have been eating products made from the flour of ground red or white acorns since Neolithic times. Dotori guksu, or Korean acorn noodles, are just one example. They are smooth, nutty, subtly sweet, and wonderfully chewy.

1 Prepare the broth. Combine the beef broth, vinegar, soy sauce, garlic, ginger, scallions, and sugar in a large stockpot and bring to a boil over medium heat. Once it's boiling, reduce the heat to a simmer and cook until the broth is reduced by ¼, about 30 minutes. Strain through a fine sieve and let cool. When cool, chill in the refrigerator for at least 2 hours.

2 Prepare the soup. Place the cucumbers in a bowl and the radishes in another bowl. Sprinkle each with ½ teaspoon of the salt, the sugar, and the vinegar and toss to coat. Place the Asian pears in another medium bowl, sprinkle with the remaining salt, and toss to coat. Let stand for 15 minutes.

3 Bring a large pot of water to a boil, add the noodles, and cook until they are tender but chewy, 5 to 7 minutes. Drain, rinse under cold water, and drain again.

4 Divide the noodles between four bowls. Pour about 1¾ cups of the broth into each bowl. Add the crushed ice and arrange the radish, cucumber, egg halves, and pears on top of the noodles. Garnish with sesame seeds and serve with the spicy mustard on the side.

INGREDIENTS

For the Broth

8 cups beef broth

⅓ cup rice vinegar

1½ tablespoons soy sauce

2 garlic cloves, peeled and thinly sliced

2-inch piece of fresh ginger, peeled and thinly sliced

4 scallions, white and light green parts only, cut into ½-inch pieces

2½ tablespoons sugar

For the Soup

2 small cucumbers, peeled and julienned

5 radishes, trimmed and very thinly sliced

1½ teaspoons salt

1 teaspoon sugar

1 teaspoon rice vinegar

2 small Asian pears, julienned

½ pound dotori guksu (Korean acorn noodles)

1 cup crushed ice

2 large hard-boiled eggs, peeled and halved lengthwise

Sesame seeds, for garnish

Spicy mustard, for serving

TIP: SINCE DOTORI GUKSU CAN BE DIFFICULT TO FIND, FEEL FREE TO USE THE LESS CHEWY BUT MORE READILY AVAILABLE SOBA NOODLES.

Coconut Curry Chicken Noodle Soup

**YIELD: 4 SERVINGS • ACTIVE TIME: 30 MINUTES
TOTAL TIME: 45 MINUTES**

This recipe uses sambal oelek, a popular Indonesian chili paste that tends to add more heat than flavor; if you can't find it, substitute Sriracha or red pepper flakes.

1 Trim the top and base of the lemongrass stalk and use only the bottom 4 inches or so, as it is the most tender part. Peel off the dry or tough outer layer and then mince the tender inner core. Bring a pot filled with water to a boil. While it comes to a boil, put the bean sprouts in a bowl of cold water. Discard the hulls that float to the top, then rinse the remaining sprouts under cold water. Add the sprouts to the boiling water and cook for 2 minutes. Remove them from the water with a strainer and immediately run them under cold water. Drain well and set aside. Keep the water at a gentle simmer.

2 Heat a Dutch oven over medium-low heat for 2 to 3 minutes. Add the oil and raise the heat to medium-high. When the oil begins to glisten, add the lemongrass, onion, ginger, and a pinch of salt and stir. When the mixture starts to gently sizzle, reduce the heat to low, cover, and cook, while stirring occasionally, until softened, about 10 minutes. Add the garlic and sambal oelek to the pan, raise the heat to medium-high, and cook, while stirring, until fragrant, about 1 minute. Add the chicken and a couple pinches of salt and stir-fry for 1 minute. Add the curry powder, stir to thoroughly coat the chicken, and then add the broth, coconut milk, cream, fish sauce, sugar, and, if using, turmeric. Stir to combine, bring to a boil, reduce the heat to low, and simmer until the chicken is completely cooked, 6 to 7 minutes. While the chicken is cooking, bring the pot of water back to a rolling boil, add the noodles, and cook until they are tender but still chewy. Drain, rinse with hot water, and drain again.

3 Divide the hot noodles between four warm bowls. Ladle the hot soup over the noodles, making sure everyone gets an equal amount of chicken. Top with a sprinkling of bean sprouts, cilantro, and scallions and serve with lime wedges and additional sambal oelek.

1 lemongrass stalk

1 cup bean sprouts, picked over, plus more for serving

2 tablespoons safflower oil

1 small onion, minced

2-inch piece of ginger, peeled and grated

Salt, to taste

2 garlic cloves, minced

1 to 2 teaspoons sambal oelek, plus more for serving

1 pound boneless, skinless chicken thighs, trimmed of any fat and cut into bite-sized pieces

2½ tablespoons curry powder

4 cups chicken broth

1 (14 oz.) can of unsweetened coconut milk

⅓ cup heavy cream

2½ tablespoons fish sauce

1½ tablespoons sugar, more to taste

½ teaspoon ground turmeric (optional)

½ pound long, thin dried rice noodles

Cilantro, chopped, for garnish

Scallions, thinly sliced, for garnish

Lime wedges, for serving

Curry Shrimp Laksa

YIELD: 6 SERVINGS • ACTIVE TIME: 20 MINUTES
TOTAL TIME: 1 HOUR

This Southeast Asian noodle soup is a wonderful combination of creamy, spicy, sweet, and salty. The basis of it is a flavor paste that is available in most well-stocked Asian markets and online.

1 Trim the top and base of the lemongrass stalk and use only the bottom 4 inches or so, as it is the most tender part. Peel off the dry or tough outer layer and then mince the tender inner core. Bring a stockpot filled with water to a boil. While it comes to a boil, put the bean sprouts in a bowl of cold water. Discard the hulls that float to the top, then rinse the remaining sprouts under cold water. Add the sprouts to the boiling water and cook for 2 minutes. Remove them from the water with a serving spoon and immediately run them under cold water. Drain well and set aside. Keep the water at a gentle simmer.

2 Heat a large skillet over medium heat for 2 to 3 minutes. Add the bok choy, two pinches of salt, and water and stir. When the water starts to boil, cover, and let steam for 2 minutes. Remove the skillet from the heat and set aside. Heat a Dutch oven over medium-low heat for 2 to 3 minutes and then add the ⅓ cup of the peanut oil (or grapeseed oil). Raise the heat to medium-high and when the oil begins to glisten, add the garlic, shallots, ginger, and a pinch of salt and stir. When the mixture sizzles, reduce the heat to low, cover, and cook, while stirring occasionally, for about 15 minutes.

3 Raise the heat to medium, add the laksa paste, and stir until very aromatic, about 1 minute. Add the lemongrass and cinnamon sticks, stir, and cook for 5 minutes. Add the coconut milk, broth, fish sauce, season with salt and pepper, and stir to combine. Bring to a boil, reduce the heat to medium low, cover, and cook until all the flavors have sufficiently blended, about 15 minutes.

4 While the soup is simmering, bring the pot of water back to a rolling boil, add the noodles, and cook until they are tender but chewy. Drain and transfer them to a medium bowl. Add the remaining peanut oil, toss, and set aside. Add the shrimp to the soup and cook until they are opaque and cooked through, about 5 minutes.

5 Divide the rice noodles between warm bowls and place the bok choy on top of them. Ladle the piping hot soup over both, making sure everyone gets an equal amount of shrimp. Top with the bean sprouts, garnish with mint, and serve with lime wedges and sambal oelek or Sriracha.

INGREDIENTS

2 lemongrass stalks

3 cups mung bean sprouts, picked over

4 bok choy, chopped

Salt and freshly ground white pepper, to taste

¼ cup water

⅓ cup peanut or grapeseed oil, plus ½ tablespoon

3 garlic cloves, peeled and minced

5 large shallots, minced

1-inch piece of ginger, peeled and grated

6 tablespoons laksa paste

2 cinnamon sticks

3 cups unsweetened coconut milk

8 cups chicken broth

2 tablespoons fish sauce

1 pound rice noodles

1 pound medium shrimp, peeled and deveined

¼ cup mint leaves, for garnish

Lime wedges, for serving

Sambal oelek or Sriracha, for serving

Pasta Soup with Cannellini Beans and Mussels

YIELD: 4 SERVINGS • ACTIVE TIME: 45 MINUTES
TOTAL TIME: 1 HOUR AND 15 MINUTES

Traditionally, this dish is half mussels, and equal parts pasta and beans. In this recipe, the ratio of mussels and pasta is adjusted, turning the dish into a lovely soup.

1 Bring the wine to a boil in a small saucepan and continue to boil until reduced almost by half, about 5 minutes. Remove from heat and set aside.

2 Bring 2 cups of water to a boil in a large stockpot. Add the mussels to the pot, cover, and reduce the heat to medium. The mussels will quickly begin to open with the heat. As they do, pluck them out with tongs and transfer to a large bowl. When the majority of the mussels have opened, discard the few that remain closed, strain the steaming liquid through a paper towel-lined fine sieve, and reserve (you should have 1½ to 2 cups). Separate the meat of the mussels from the shells, transfer the meat to a

small bowl, and discard the shells. Rinse and dry the stockpot and return it to the burner.

3 Place the beans in a medium bowl and mash until approximately half of the beans are mashed. Set aside.

4 Heat the stockpot over medium heat for 2 to 3 minutes. Add the olive oil and heat for 1 to 2 minutes. Once it begins to glisten, add the onion and a couple pinches of salt and stir. Once the onion begins to sizzle, reduce the heat to low, cover, and cook, stirring occasionally, until very soft, about 20 minutes.

5 Add the garlic and red pepper flakes, raise the heat to medium-high, and cook until fragrant, about 1 minute. Stir in the fish sauce, cook for another minute, and then add the broth, beans, tomatoes, rosemary stem, and the reserved mussel broth. Stir, season to taste with salt and pepper, and bring to a boil. Add the pasta, cook until tender but chewy, and then add the mussel meat. Stir until it is heated through.

6 Ladle the soup into warm bowls and garnish with the rosemary leaves and parsley.

INGREDIENTS

2 cups dry white wine

2 pounds mussels, scrubbed and debearded

1 (14 oz.) can of cannellini beans, rinsed and drained

2 tablespoons extra virgin olive oil

1 white onion, finely diced

Salt and black pepper, to taste

3 garlic cloves, peeled and minced

1 teaspoon red pepper flakes

1 tablespoon fish sauce

6 cups chicken or vegetable broth

1 (14 oz.) can of diced tomatoes, with their juice

1 sprig of fresh rosemary, leaves chopped, stem reserved

½ pound pasta

Handful of parsley, chopped, for garnish

Pasta E Fagioli

YIELD: 8 SERVINGS • ACTIVE TIME: 30 MINUTES
TOTAL TIME: 1½ HOURS

This soup has a prominent role in many Italian-American restaurants in the United States, while in Italy it is considered too simple to be served to guests.

INGREDIENTS

2 tablespoons extra virgin olive oil, plus more for drizzling

1 pound pork spareribs, cut into 4 pieces along the bones

Salt and black pepper, to taste

4 oz. pancetta or bacon, finely chopped

1 onion, minced

1 celery stalk, minced

3 carrots, chopped

3 garlic cloves, peeled and thinly sliced

3 oil-packed anchovy fillets

1 (14 oz.) can of peeled San Marzano tomatoes, with their juice, crushed by hand

1 piece of Parmesan cheese rind (optional)

3 (14 oz.) cans of cannellini beans, drained and rinsed

6½ cups chicken broth

½ pound pasta

¼ cup parsley, chopped, for garnish

1 cup Parmesan cheese, grated, for garnish

1 Heat a large pot or Dutch oven over medium heat for 2 to 3 minutes. Add the olive oil, raise the heat to medium-high, and heat for 1 to 2 minutes. As the oil heats, blot the sparerib pieces with paper towels to absorb as much surface moisture as possible and then season them with salt and pepper. Add them and the pancetta (or bacon) to the pot once the oil begins to glisten. Cook, while turning the spareribs over every couple of minutes, until they are golden brown, 6 to 8 minutes. Transfer the spareribs to a plate and reduce the heat to medium.

2 Add the onion, celery, carrots, and a couple pinches of salt, and cook, while stirring occasionally, until the vegetables begin to gently sizzle. Cover and cook, while stirring occasionally, until the vegetables are very soft, about 20 minutes.

3 Add the garlic and anchovies and cook, while stirring constantly, until the anchovies dissolve, about 1 minute. Add the tomatoes and their juice and a couple pinches of salt and scrape up any browned bits from the bottom of the pot. Raise the heat to medium-high, and add the cheese rind (if using), beans, broth, and ½ teaspoon salt, and bring to a boil. Reduce the heat to low and cook, while stirring occasionally, until the flavors blend together, about 45 minutes. Discard the cheese rind and return the spareribs to the pot.

4 Add the pasta and cook until tender but still chewy, about 10 minutes. Remove the pot from heat, season to taste, ladle into warm bowls, and top with a drizzle of olive oil, the parsley, and Parmesan.

Chicken Soup with Meatballs, Farfalle, and Spinach

YIELD: 8 SERVINGS • ACTIVE TIME: 35 MINUTES
TOTAL TIME: 1 HOUR AND 15 MINUTES

Here, farfalle are paired with small, savory meatballs and vegetables to create a delicious one-pot soup that is capable of warming the whole family.

INGREDIENTS

For the Meatballs

½ of a stale baguette, broken into pieces

1 pound ground chicken

½ cup soft bread crumbs

1 cup Parmesan cheese, grated

3 tablespoons tomato paste

Handful of parsley, chopped

3 large eggs

Salt and black pepper, to taste

Peanut oil, for frying

For the Soup

2 leeks, white and light green parts only, trimmed and chopped

2 tablespoons extra virgin olive oil

Salt and black pepper, to taste

5 garlic cloves, peeled and thinly sliced

8 cups chicken broth

5 carrots, sliced into ½-inch-thick rounds

½ pound farfalle

2 handfuls of baby spinach leaves, stemmed

¼ cup Parmesan cheese, grated, plus more for garnish

1 Prepare the meatballs. Place the baguette pieces in a medium bowl and cover with water. Soak for 15 minutes, turning the pieces over twice. Squeeze as much of the liquid as possible from the bread and remove any hard pieces of crust that remain. Place the squeezed bread in a large bowl. Add the chicken, bread crumbs, Parmesan, tomato paste, parsley, and eggs, season with salt and pepper, and stir until well combined. Form the mixture into 45 to 50 ½-inch balls, heat a large skillet over medium heat for 2 to 3 minutes, and then add just enough oil to completely cover the bottom. Working in batches, add the meatballs in a single layer and cook until they are golden brown all over, 6 to 8 minutes. Transfer them to a paper towel-lined plate.

2 Prepare the soup. Place the leeks in a large bowl of water and swish them around to remove any dirt. Drain well, transfer to a kitchen towel, and set aside.

3 Heat a Dutch oven over medium heat for 2 to 3 minutes. Add the olive oil, heat for 1 to 2 minutes, and then add the leeks.

Season with salt and pepper. When the leeks start to sizzle, reduce the heat to low, cover, and cook, while stirring occasionally, until the leeks are very soft, about 15 minutes. Add the garlic, cook for another minute, and then add the broth, carrots, farfalle, and meatballs and bring to a gentle boil. Cook over medium-low heat for 15 minutes.

4 Remove the Dutch oven from heat and add the spinach and Parmesan. Stir to combine and let stand for 5 minutes so the spinach wilts. Stir, ladle into warm bowls, and garnish with additional Parmesan.

TIP: MATZO BALLS OR CHICKEN MEATBALLS MAKE FOR A LOVELY ADDITION TO THIS SOUP.

INGREDIENTS

For the Stock

1 tablespoon olive oil

5 pounds skin-on, bone-in chicken thighs, trimmed

Salt and black pepper, to taste

12 chicken necks (or 4 chicken feet), trimmed

4 chicken backs, trimmed

3 celery stalks

2 carrots, cut into large pieces

1 leek, trimmed, washed well, and cut into pieces

1 medium yellow onion, halved

3 garlic cloves, smashed and peel left on

12 cups water

Handful of fresh parsley

2 bay leaves

4 cups crushed tomatoes

10 black peppercorns

For the Soup

Reserved shredded chicken

5 carrots, chopped into ¼-inch pieces

5 celery stalks, chopped into ¼-inch pieces

Salt and black pepper, to taste

4 cups warm egg noodles, cooked

Dill, chopped, for garnish

Penicillin Soup with Egg Noodles

YIELD: 8 SERVINGS • ACTIVE TIME: 1 HOUR AND 15 MINUTES
TOTAL TIME: 3½ HOURS TO 4½ HOURS

If you are sick, or you're just having one of those days where you wished you had stayed in bed, this soup is guaranteed to bring a smile to your face.

1 Prepare the stock. Heat a stockpot over medium heat for 2 minutes and add the olive oil. As the oil heats, season half of the chicken thighs with salt and pepper. Once the oil begins to glisten, add them to the pan, skin side down. Reduce the heat slightly so the thighs gently sizzle and cook for 5 minutes without moving them. Flip and cook the other side for another 5 minutes. Transfer the thighs to a platter. Repeat with the remaining thighs, chicken necks (or feet), and chicken backs.

2 Add the vegetables and garlic to the pot and cook until browned, 12 to 15 minutes. Add ½ cup of the water and scrape up the browned bits from the bottom of the pot. Return the chicken pieces to the pot and add the remaining water, along with the parsley, bay leaves, tomatoes, and peppercorns. Stir to combine, bring to a boil, and then reduce the heat to a simmer. Use a wide spoon to skim off the foam that rises to the surface. Cook for 2 to 3 hours; the longer you cook it, the more flavorful the stock becomes. Once cooled, strain the stock into another stockpot through a fine sieve. Separate the cooked chicken meat from the bones, shred it, and set aside.

3 Prepare the soup. Bring the stock to a gentle boil over medium heat. Add the shredded chicken, carrots, and celery. Stir to combine and cook until the carrots and celery are tender, about 15 minutes. Season to taste with salt and pepper, and place ½ cup of cooked egg noodles in each bowl. Ladle the soup over the noodles, garnish with dill, and serve.

Ditalini and Chickpea Soup

YIELD: 4 SERVINGS • ACTIVE TIME: 15 MINUTES
TOTAL TIME: 16 HOURS

This simple Italian soup is perfect for your vegan friends or family members. Ditalini is a small, tube-shaped pasta.

INGREDIENTS

1¼ dried chickpeas, soaked overnight

6 cups water, plus more as needed

1 tablespoon dried kombu seaweed

3 garlic cloves

2 tablespoons extra virgin olive oil, plus more for garnish

2 sprigs of rosemary, 1 left whole, leaves removed and chopped from the other

1 cup ditalini

Salt and pepper, to taste

1 Rinse the chickpeas and then place in a medium saucepan. Cover with the water, add the seaweed and the garlic, and bring to a simmer. Cook for 2 hours, or until the chickpeas are nice and tender.

2 Reserve ¼ of the cooked chickpeas. Transfer the remaining contents of the saucepan to a food processor and puree.

3 In a medium saucepan, add the olive oil and warm over medium-high heat.

4 Gently place the whole rosemary sprig into the pan and cook for a few minutes, until it is soft and fragrant. Remove the rosemary sprig and discard. Add the chickpea puree and reserved chickpeas. Add the pasta and cook for 10 minutes. If the soup becomes too thick, add more water.

5 Add the chopped rosemary, season with salt and pepper, and ladle into warm bowls. Garnish with a splash of olive oil.

Italian Wedding Soup

YIELD: 4 SERVINGS • ACTIVE TIME: 30 MINUTES
TOTAL TIME: 1 HOUR AND 15 MINUTES

The term wedding soup comes from the phrase *minestra maritata*, which means "married soup," a reference to the beautiful combination of leafy greens and meat.

1 Prepare the meatballs. Preheat oven to 350°F. In a bowl, add all the ingredients and mix with a fork until well combined. Divide the mixture into 16 balls, roll with your hands until nice and round, and then place on a baking sheet.

2 Place the sheet in oven and bake for 20 to 25 minutes, until nicely browned and cooked through. Remove from the oven and set aside.

3 Prepare the soup. In a medium saucepan, add the olive oil and cook over medium heat until warm. Add the onion, carrots, and celery and cook for 5 minutes, or until soft. Add the stock and the wine and bring to a boil. Reduce heat so that the soup simmers, add the pasta, and cook for 8 minutes.

4 Add the cooked meatballs and simmer for 5 minutes. Add the dill and the spinach and cook for 2 minutes, or until the spinach has wilted. Season with salt and pepper, ladle into warm bowls, and garnish with the Parmesan.

INGREDIENTS

For the Meatballs

12 oz. ground chicken

⅓ cup panko bread crumbs

1 garlic clove, minced

2 tablespoons parsley, chopped

¼ cup Parmesan cheese, grated

1 tablespoon milk

1 egg, beaten

⅛ teaspoon fennel seeds

⅛ teaspoon red pepper flakes

½ teaspoon paprika

Salt and pepper, to taste

For the Soup

2 tablespoons extra virgin olive oil

1 onion, chopped

2 carrots, minced

1 celery stalk, minced

6 cups chicken stock

¼ cup white wine

½ cup pasta

2 tablespoons dill, chopped

6 oz. baby spinach

Salt and pepper, to taste

Parmesan cheese, grated, for garnish

Chicken Parm Soup

YIELD: 4 SERVINGS • ACTIVE TIME: 20 MINUTES
TOTAL TIME: 1 HOUR

By turning this famous Italian-American dish into a soup, your work in the kitchen is certain to garner a few devotees.

INGREDIENTS

2 tablespoons extra virgin olive oil

2 chicken breasts, cut into ½-inch pieces

1 onion, chopped

2 garlic cloves, minced

1 teaspoon red pepper flakes

¼ cup tomato paste

1 (14 oz.) can of diced stewed tomatoes

6 cups chicken stock

2 cups penne

2 cups mozzarella, shredded

1 cup Parmesan cheese, grated, plus more for garnish

Salt and pepper, to taste

Basil, chopped, for garnish

1 In a medium saucepan, add the oil and warm over medium-high heat. Add the chicken and cook for 5 minutes, while turning, until golden brown. Add the onion and garlic and cook for 5 minutes, or until the onion is soft.

2 Add the red pepper flakes, tomato paste, tomatoes, and stock and bring to a boil. Reduce heat so that the soup simmers and cook for 10 minutes.

3 Add the penne and cook for 12 minutes. Add the mozzarella and Parmesan and stir until they melt. Season with salt and pepper, ladle into warm bowls, and garnish with basil and additional Parmesan.

In the Oven

Freighted with melted cheese and creamy sauce, the noodle dishes that come together in the oven are the ultimate indulgence. If you're one of the few who didn't turn to this chapter immediately, whip up a Classic Lasagna with Bolognese and Béchamel (see pages 180–181) or some Baked Ziti (see pages 184–185) and you'll see why an oven-based preparation is so often people's response when asked to choose their favorite pasta dish. While most traditional baked preparations utilize ricotta cheese, we've focused on recipes that utilize béchamel sauce in this section, believing that it guards against the dishes becoming overly dry as they cook.

Classic Lasagna with Bolognese and Béchamel

YIELD: 10 SERVINGS • ACTIVE TIME: 2 HOURS
TOTAL TIME: 3 HOURS

The luxurious béchamel sauce, egg pasta, savory meat sauce, and grated Parmesan combine to create a lasagna that is both stick-to-your-ribs satisfying and surprisingly light.

INGREDIENTS

All Yolk Pasta Dough (see pages 24–25), rolled to ¹⁄₁₆-inch thick and cut into 1-foot-long pieces; or 1½ pounds dried lasagna noodles

Salt, to taste

Bolognese Sauce (see page 57)

Béchamel Sauce (see page 82)

2 cups Parmesan cheese, grated

1 Bring a large pot of water to a boil. Once it's boiling, add salt (1 tablespoon for every 4 cups water) and stir. Add the pasta sheets, only one or two at a time, and boil them until still very firm (1 to 2 minutes for fresh pasta and about 5 to 6 minutes for dried lasagna sheets). Transfer the cooked sheets to a large bowl of cold water, allow them to cool completely, then arrange them in a single layer on clean, damp kitchen towels.

2 Cover the bottom of a 15 x 10-inch baking pan with the bolognese. Arrange a single layer of the cooked noodles over the sauce, making sure they are slightly overlapping one another. Then cover the noodles with bolognese. Dollop a quarter or so of the béchamel sauce on the bolognese and gently spread it over the meat sauce. Evenly sprinkle over ½ cup of the cheese. Repeat this layering process until the lasagna is about ½ inch or so from the top of the baking dish. Spread a thin layer of bolognese over the top layer of noodles and sprinkle with the remaining cheese. Cover loosely with aluminum foil and bake or refrigerate for up to a day, bringing it back to room temperature before baking.

3 Preheat the oven to 375°F. Put the lasagna in the oven and bake for 45 minutes. Remove the foil and continue baking until the top is crusty around the edges, about another 20 minutes or so. For nice, clean slices, allow the lasagna to rest for at least 30 minutes before cutting into it.

Porcini Mushroom and Béchamel Lasagna

YIELD: 6 SERVINGS • ACTIVE TIME: 1 HOUR
TOTAL TIME: 2 HOURS

Bewitching and earthy porcini mushrooms and lemony, minty thyme pool their considerable talents to make this exceptional lasagna.

1 Place the porcini mushrooms in a small bowl with the water and soak until they have softened, about 15 minutes. Lightly run your fingers across all the pieces to dislodge any dirt or debris. Gather them in your hand and gently squeeze over the bowl to remove excess water, then chop. Strain the soaking liquid through a paper towel-lined sieve and reserve 1½ cups. Set aside.

2 Bring the wine to a boil in a small saucepan and continue to boil until reduced almost by half, about 5 minutes. Remove from heat and set aside.

3 Heat a large, deep skillet over medium heat for 2 to 3 minutes and add the butter. When the butter melts, add the shallots and a pinch of salt and stir.

Once the shallots begin to gently sizzle, reduce the temperature to low, cover, and cook, stirring occasionally, until they have softened, about 10 minutes. Stir in the garlic and cook for 30 seconds. Raise the heat to medium-high, add the mushrooms and thyme, season with salt, and stir. Cook, while stirring frequently, until the mushrooms begin to soften and release their liquid, about 6 minutes. Add the reduced wine, the porcini soaking liquid, and a pinch of salt and bring to a gentle boil. Continue to cook on medium-high heat, while stirring occasionally, until the mushrooms are tender and the liquid has reduced by half, 12 to 15 minutes. Remove from heat, season to taste, add the béchamel, and stir until well combined.

4 Preheat the oven to 350°F. Bring a large pot of water to a boil. Once it's boiling, add salt (1 tablespoon for every 4 cups water) and stir. Add the pasta sheets, only one or two at a time, and boil them until still very firm (1 to 2 minutes for fresh pasta and about 5 to 6 minutes for dried lasagna sheets). Transfer the cooked sheets to a large bowl of cold water, allow them to cool completely, then arrange them in a single layer on clean, damp kitchen towels.

5 Cover the bottom of a deep 9 x 13-inch baking dish with the mushroom sauce. Cover with a layer of noodles, making sure they are slightly overlapping one another. Then spoon enough sauce to cover the first layer of noodles evenly and sprinkle with ½ cup of the Parmesan. Repeat this layering two more times, ending with a layer of the mushroom sauce topped with the remaining Parmesan. Cover loosely with aluminum foil, place in the oven, and bake for 35 minutes. Remove the foil and continue to bake until the edges of the lasagna sheets are lightly browned, about 12 minutes. For nice, clean slices, allow the lasagna to rest for at least 20 minutes before slicing.

INGREDIENTS

1 oz. dried porcini mushrooms

2 cups warm water

1 cup dry red wine

2 tablespoons unsalted butter

3 shallots, minced

Salt and black pepper, to taste

2 garlic cloves, peeled and minced

1 pound cremini mushrooms, stemmed and thinly sliced

2 sprigs of fresh thyme, leaves chopped, plus more for garnish

½ recipe Béchamel Sauce (see page 82)

½ recipe of All Yolk Pasta Dough (see pages 24–25), rolled to 1/16-inch thick and cut into 1-foot-long pieces; or ½ pound dried lasagna noodles

2 cups Parmesan cheese, grated

VARIATION: THE TENDER TEXTURE OF EGG PASTA LENDS ITSELF MARVELOUSLY TO THIS RECIPE; HOWEVER, TO SAVE AN HOUR'S WORTH OF WORK TO MAKE THE LASAGNA SHEETS FROM SCRATCH, USING NO-BOIL LASAGNA NOODLES WILL ALSO YIELD WONDERFUL RESULTS.

Baked Ziji

YIELD: 6 SERVINGS • ACTIVE TIME: 40 MINUTES
TOTAL TIME: 1½ HOURS

Though fish sauce is nowhere near traditional in this Italian-American classic, you'll find yourself wondering how you ever lived without the deep savory notes it adds to the sauce.

1 Heat a large skillet over medium-low heat for 2 to 3 minutes. Add the olive oil and raise the heat to medium. When the oil begins to glisten, add the pancetta. Cook, while stirring often, until the pancetta is golden brown, 4 to 5 minutes. Raise the heat to medium-high and add the onion, a couple pinches of salt, and the red pepper flakes. When the mixture begins to gently sizzle, reduce the heat to low, cover, and cook until the onion has become very soft, about 15 minutes.

2 Raise the heat to medium-high, stir in the tomato paste and fish sauce, and cook, while stirring, until the mixture has slightly darkened, about 2 minutes. Add the tomatoes, sugar, and a couple pinches of salt and stir. Bring the sauce to a gentle boil, reduce the heat to low, cover, and cook, while stirring often, until the sauce is slightly reduced, about 30 minutes. Season to taste with salt and pepper.

3 Preheat the oven to 350°F. Butter the sides and bottom of 9 x 13-inch baking dish. Combine the béchamel and the mozzarella in a large bowl. Bring a large pot of water to a boil. Once it's boiling, add salt (1 tablespoon for every 4 cups water) and stir. Add the pasta and cook for half of the directed time. Drain and immediately add to the bowl containing the béchamel and mozzarella. Add 1 cup of the Parmesan and toss to coat.

4 Add all but 1½ cups of the tomato sauce to the bowl and gently fold the mixture a few times, leaving streaks of béchamel. Transfer the mixture to the prepared baking dish and top with the remaining tomato sauce and Parmesan. Bake for 15 to 20 minutes and then turn the broiler on and broil the pasta, until dark caramel-colored spots begin to develop on the surface, about 4 minutes. Remove from the oven and let sit for 15 minutes before serving on warm plates, garnished with a sprinkling of basil.

INGREDIENTS

2 tablespoons extra virgin olive oil

2 oz. pancetta, diced

1 large yellow onion, chopped

Salt, to taste

2 teaspoons red pepper flakes

1 tablespoon tomato paste

1 tablespoon fish sauce

3 (14 oz.) cans of peeled San Marzano tomatoes, pureed

¼ teaspoon sugar

1½ tablespoons unsalted butter

½ recipe Béchamel Sauce (see page 82)

1 pound room-temperature fresh mozzarella cheese, cut into ½-inch cubes

1 pound ziti

2½ cups Parmesan cheese, grated

Handful of basil, chopped, for garnish

Cannelloni with Butternut Squash, Ricotta, and Sage

YIELD: 9 TO 10 SERVINGS • ACTIVE TIME: 1 HOUR
TOTAL TIME: 2 HOURS

Literally "large reeds" in Italian, cannelloni are thin sheets of pasta rolled around a savory filling. In this recipe, they encase the classic combination of butternut squash and sage, enriched by creamy ricotta.

1 Preheat the oven to 400°F. Use a spoon to scrape out the seeds and fibrous insides of the squash. Prick the flesh with a fork, brush all the cut surfaces lightly with 1 tablespoon of the olive oil and place, cut side down, on a parchment-lined baking sheet. Place on the center rack of the oven, reduce the temperature to 375°F, and roast until you can easily pierce the squash with a fork, 40 to 45 minutes. Remove from the oven and let cool. When cool enough to handle, scoop the soft flesh out of the skins and mash until smooth.

2 Heat a large skillet over low for 2 to 3 minutes. Add 2 tablespoons of the oil and the garlic and raise the heat to medium. Once it just starts to turn golden brown,

remove the skillet from heat and transfer the garlic and oil to the bowl with the squash. Add the cheeses, half of the sage, the nutmeg, season with salt and pepper, and stir until well combined. Use or cover and refrigerate for up to 3 days.

3 Bring a large pot of water to a boil. Once it's boiling, add salt (1 tablespoon for every 4 cups water) and stir. Add the squares of pasta and cook until they are just tender, about 2 minutes. Drain, rinse under cold water, and toss with ½ tablespoon of oil to prevent them from sticking.

4 Generously oil a baking dish large enough to fit all the filled cannelloni in a single layer. To fill the cannelloni, place a pasta square in front of you. Place ¼

INGREDIENTS

2 pounds butternut squash,
ends trimmed and halved

5½ tablespoons extra virgin olive oil

5 garlic cloves, peeled and minced

1½ cups whole-milk ricotta cheese

1 cup Parmesan cheese, grated

12 fresh sage leaves, thinly sliced

1 teaspoon nutmeg, grated

Salt and white pepper, to taste

All Yolk Pasta Dough (see pages 24–25),
rolled ⅟₁₆-inch thick and cut into
5-inch squares

Browned Butter and Sage Sauce
(see page 60)

cup of the squash mixture in the center of the square and shape it into a rough cylinder. Roll the pasta square into a tube around the filling and transfer to the prepared baking dish, seam side down. Repeat with remaining squares and filling. When the baking dish is filled, brush the cannelloni tops with the remaining 2 tablespoons of oil.

5 Preheat the oven to 375°F. Put the baking dish on a center rack and bake until the cannelloni are very hot and begin to turn golden brown, about 20 minutes. Drizzle with the sauce and sprinkle with the remaining sage before serving.

Vegetarian Rotolo with Gingery Red Pepper Sauce

YIELD: 6 SERVINGS • ACTIVE TIME: 1 HOUR AND 15 MINUTES
TOTAL TIME: 1½ HOURS

A tantalizing mash-up of pasta and delicious, aromatic Asian flavors. Make sure you keep the recipe for the sauce close by, as your loved ones will be constantly clamoring for it.

1 Prepare the sauce. Place all of the ingredients in a food processor and pulse until smooth. Transfer to a small saucepan and cook over medium heat until it has the consistency of a nice, thick tomato sauce, about 20 minutes. You can prepare this sauce in advance and refrigerate for up to 3 days.

2 Fill a very large bowl with cold water and add the vinegar. Add the mushrooms and swirl them around in the water for 30 seconds or so. Transfer them to a colander and rinse under cold water. Drain well and place them on a kitchen towel, stem side down. Let air-dry for 30 minutes, then mince.

3 Place the tofu in a single layer on a paper towel-lined tray. Cover with paper towels and pat dry. Let them sit for 30 minutes, changing the paper towels after 15 minutes. Chop and set aside.

4 Heat a large skillet over medium heat for 2 to 3 minutes. Add the peanut oil and heat for 1 to 2 minutes. When it begins to glisten, add the scallions and a pinch of salt and cook, while stirring occasionally, for 3 to 4 minutes. Raise the heat to medium-high, add the mushrooms, tofu, cabbage, and carrots, season with salt, and cook, while stirring frequently, until the cabbage has wilted slightly, about 5 minutes.

INGREDIENTS

For the Sauce

2 red bell peppers, seeded and roughly chopped

1-inch piece of ginger, peeled and roughly chopped

4 garlic cloves, peeled

3 tablespoons sugar

2 tablespoons tomato paste

1 tablespoon extra virgin olive oil

1 tablespoon apple cider vinegar

1 tablespoon soy sauce

For the Rotolo

1 tablespoon distilled white vinegar

1 pound cremini mushrooms, stemmed

1 pound extra firm tofu, drained and cut into ½-inch slices

5 tablespoons peanut oil

10 scallions, white and light green parts only, thinly sliced

Salt, to taste

4 cups cabbage, shredded

4 carrots, peeled and grated

3 tablespoons soy sauce

3 tablespoons water

2 tablespoons sugar

1 teaspoon freshly ground white pepper

4 teaspoons toasted sesame oil, plus more for greasing the pan

4 teaspoons cornstarch

All Yolk Pasta Dough
(see pages 24–25), rolled 1/16-inch thick and cut into 15-inch-long sheets

2 handfuls of cilantro, chopped, plus more for garnish

Continued...

5 While the vegetables cook, whisk the soy sauce, 2 tablespoons of the water, the sugar, pepper, and sesame oil together in a small bowl. In another small bowl, whisk the cornstarch with the remaining water until smooth, then whisk it into the soy mixture. Stir this into the vegetables and raise the heat to high. Cook until the liquid evaporates and the vegetables are cooked through, about 2 minutes. Remove from heat and let cool slightly, then transfer to a food processor. Pulse several times until you have a rough puree. Season to taste and use or cover and refrigerate for up to 2 days.

6 Bring a large pot of water to a boil. Once it's boiling, add salt (1 tablespoon for every 4 cups water) and stir, then add a single sheet of pasta. Cook for a minute, then carefully retrieve the sheet using two large slotted spoons. Transfer to a kitchen towel laid out flat on the kitchen counter and let cool. Repeat the process until all the pasta sheets are cooked.

7 Preheat the oven to 475°F. Generously grease a 15 x 10-inch baking pan with sesame oil. Work with one pasta sheet at a time. Lay it on a work surface covered with parchment paper. Using a rubber spatula, spread the filling over the sheet and sprinkle with a small amount of the cilantro. Starting at one short end, roll the sheet up tightly. Once you are done rolling, rest it on its seam to keep it from unrolling, or you can secure the end with a couple of toothpicks. Repeat with the remaining pasta sheets, filling, and cilantro. Using a very sharp knife, slice each pasta roll into $1\frac{1}{4}$ inch-thick rounds. Arrange them, cut side down, in the prepared baking dish, leaving $\frac{1}{4}$ inch between the pieces. Put the pan in the oven and bake until lightly browned on top and heated through, 10 to 12 minutes. Place 2 to 3 tablespoons of piping hot sauce on a warm plate, arrange three rotolo slices on top, sprinkle with additional cilantro, and serve.

TIP: IF YOU WOULD PREFER TO NOT MAKE YOUR OWN PASTA, PURCHASE A BOX OF DRIED PASTA SHEETS, COOK THEM FOR HALF OF THE SUGGESTED TIME, AND THEN OVERLAP THEM SLIGHTLY TO ACHIEVE 15 INCHES IN LENGTH BEFORE ROLLING THEM.

Pasta with Fresh Sardines

**YIELD: 4 SERVINGS • ACTIVE TIME: 45 MINUTES
TOTAL TIME: 1½ HOURS**

No other pasta dish exhibits the savory-sweet flavors featured in Sicilian cuisine quite like this one, which is known as *pasta con le sarde* in the old country.

1 Wash the sardine fillets under cold water and pat dry with paper towels. Chop half of the fillets into 1-inch pieces and leave the remainder whole.

2 Place the raisins in a small bowl, cover with warm water, and soak for 10 minutes. Drain and transfer to a paper towel-lined plate to drain.

3 Heat a small skillet over medium-low heat for 2 minutes. Add the pine nuts and cook, while stirring frequently, for 3 to 4 minutes. Remove from the heat and sprinkle with salt. Bring a large pot of water to a boil. When it's boiling, add the fennel fronds and boil for 1 minute.

Remove them from the water using a strainer, drain well, pat dry with paper towels, and chop. Keep the water at a low simmer.

4 Heat a large skillet over low heat for 1 to 2 minutes. Add 3 tablespoons of the olive oil and raise the heat to medium. Once it begins to glisten, add the onion and a couple pinches of salt and cook, while stirring occasionally, until soft but not golden, about 10 minutes. Add the raisins and pine nuts, cook for another 3 minutes, and then add the blanched fennel and a pinch of salt and stir. Reduce the heat to low, cover, and cook, while stirring occasionally, until the onion becomes very soft, about 15 minutes. If the mixture begins to look too dry, add 1 or 2 tablespoons of the simmering water.

5 Preheat the oven to 400°F and grease a deep 9 x 13-inch baking dish with oil. Add the anchovies, chopped sardines, and fennel seeds to the skillet with the onion mixture and cook, while stirring frequently, until the anchovies have completely dissolved, about 10 minutes.

6 While that cooks, bring the water back to a boil. Once it's boiling, add salt (1 tablespoon for every 4 cups) and stir. Add the spaghetti and cook 2 minutes less than the directed cooking time. Drain and reserve ¼ cup of the pasta water. Transfer the pasta to the skillet, add the reserved pasta water, and toss well. Transfer the mixture to the prepared baking dish, top with the whole sardine fillets, drizzle with the remaining 2 tablespoons oil, and season with pepper. Cover with aluminum foil, place it in the oven, and bake until the sardines have turned beige, about 15 minutes.

INGREDIENTS

1½ pounds fresh sardine fillets

½ cup golden raisins

⅓ cup pine nuts

Salt and black pepper, to taste

Handful of fennel fronds

5 tablespoons extra virgin olive oil, plus more for greasing the baking dish

1 small yellow onion, sliced into thin half-moons

5 oil-packed anchovy fillets, chopped

½ teaspoon fennel seeds

¾ pound spaghetti

INGREDIENTS

2 tablespoons extra virgin olive oil

1 yellow onion, thinly sliced

Salt and black pepper, to taste

3 zucchini, minced

¾ pound large shell pasta

¼ cup bread crumbs

½ pound mozzarella cheese, grated

½ pound thick-cut honey ham, minced

Béchamel Sauce (see page 82)

1½ cups Parmesan cheese, grated

Baked Shells with Zucchini, Ham, and Béchamel Sauce

YIELD: 6 SERVINGS • ACTIVE TIME: 1 HOUR
TOTAL TIME: 1 HOUR AND 45 MINUTES

Savory and moist, this baked dish stars lumaconi, the seashell-shaped pasta that is so hefty that three or four are generally all you will need for a filling meal.

1 Heat a large skillet over medium heat for 2 to 3 minutes, then add the olive oil. When the oil begins to glisten, add the onion and a couple pinches of salt. Cook for about 10 minutes, while stirring occasionally. Add the zucchini, season with salt, and cook, while stirring occasionally, until it is cooked through, about 10 minutes. Remove from heat and let cool.

2 Bring a large pot of water to a boil. Once it's boiling, add salt (1 tablespoon for every 4 cups water) and stir. Add the pasta and cook for ¾ of the time instructed on the package. Drain, rinse under cold water, and place in a single layer on kitchen towels to drain.

3 Preheat the oven to 375°F. Combine the zucchini mixture, bread crumbs, mozzarella, ham, and 1 cup of the béchamel in a large bowl, season to taste, and gently stir until combined. Divide the mixture between the cooked shells. Spread ¾ cup of the sauce over the bottom of a baking dish large enough to accommodate the pasta in a single layer. Add the filled shells and pour the remaining sauce over the top. Sprinkle evenly with the Parmesan and cover the dish with aluminum foil.

4 Place the dish in the oven and lower the temperature to 350°F. Bake for 20 minutes, then remove the foil and bake until the tops of the shells just start to turn golden brown, about 10 minutes.

Sagne Chine

YIELD: 10 TO 12 SERVINGS • ACTIVE TIME: 3 HOURS
TOTAL TIME: 4 HOURS

Typical of the rustic and robust cuisine found in the southern Italian region of Calabria, this is a delectable layering of pasta squares, small meatballs, hard-boiled eggs, and cheese.

1 Place the pork, bread crumbs, 1 cup of the pecorino, parsley, salt, pepper, and egg in a large bowl and use your hands to combine them. Heat the olive oil in a small skillet. When the oil starts glistening, shape 1 tablespoon of the mixture into a patty and fry for a minute on each side. Remove the skillet from the stove and let the sample cool. Taste it and determine whether you need to adjust the seasoning. When the seasoning is right, roll the mixture into ½-inch balls and set them aside.

2 Return the skillet to the stove and let the oil warm for a couple of minutes. When it starts glistening, add about ⅓ of the meatballs to the pan. Stir them around with a wooden spatula until they are nice and golden on all sides, 5 to 6 minutes total. Transfer to a plate lined with paper towels to absorb any excess oil. Repeat with the remaining meatballs.

3 Place the tomato sauce in a Dutch oven over medium heat, add the meatballs, bring to a gentle simmer, and cook for 10 minutes. Use a ladle to remove 1½ cups of the sauce and reserve. Add the frozen peas to the pot and cook until they are tender, about 5 minutes. Remove the pot from the heat.

4 Bring a large pot of water to a boil. Once it's boiling, add salt (1 tablespoon for every 4 cups water) and stir. Cook in batches, adding 2 or 3 pasta sheets at a time, and cook until they are just tender, about 1½ minutes. Drain, rinse under cold water, and lay out on a kitchen towel so they are not touching. Grease the bottom and sides of a 9 x 13-inch baking dish with a little tomato sauce.

5 Preheat the oven to 425°F. Line the bottom and sides of the dish with pasta sheets, arranging them so that 5 inches of the sheets are hanging over the side of the baking dish (they will be eventually folded over the top layer of filling). Ladle ¼ of the meatball-and-tomato sauce mixture evenly over the bottom of the dish. Layer ¼ of the egg slices on top, followed by the mozzarella and then ¼ cup of the pecorino. Cover the filling with more pasta sheets and repeat the layering process two more times.

6 Place a final pasta sheet on top. Fold over all the overhanging pasta sheets and make sure that the filling is completely covered. Spread the reserved tomato sauce over the top. Place the dish in the oven and bake until it is bubbling and puffy in the center, about 40 minutes. To be able to cut into clean slices, let the dish rest for 30 minutes.

TIP: WHEN PURCHASING MOZZARELLA FOR THE DISH, BE SURE TO BUY A RECTANGULAR BLOCK OF CHEESE, NOT THE WATER-PACKED VARIETY, AS IT WILL RELEASE TOO MUCH WATER INTO THE DISH.

INGREDIENTS

1 pound ground pork

⅔ cup bread crumbs

1¾ cups pecorino Romano cheese, grated

2 handfuls of parsley, chopped

2 teaspoons salt, plus more to taste

1 teaspoon black pepper

1 large egg

1 tablespoon extra virgin olive oil

8 cups Classic Fresh Tomato Sauce (see page 51)

1 pound frozen petite peas

All Yolk Pasta Dough (see pages 24–25), rolled 1/16-inch thick and cut into foot-long sheets; or 1 pound store-bought fresh egg pasta sheets

6 hard-boiled eggs, thinly sliced

1 pound mozzarella cheese, thinly sliced

Pastitsio

YIELD: 8 TO 10 SERVINGS • ACTIVE TIME: 1½ HOURS
TOTAL TIME: 3½ HOURS

This version of the Greek classic provides the white sauce with a bigger-than-usual role in order to lend the dish additional moisture.

1 Prepare the meat sauce. Heat a large, deep skillet over medium heat for 2 to 3 minutes. Add the olive oil and heat for 1 to 2 minutes, then add the onions and a couple pinches of salt. Reduce the heat to low, cover, and cook, while stirring occasionally, for about 20 minutes. Add the garlic, cook for 1 minute, raise the heat to medium-high, and add the lamb, pressing down on it with a wooden spoon to break it up. Cook, while stirring occasionally, until the meat is brown and cooked through, 8 to 10 minutes. Add the milk and cook until all the liquid has evaporated, about 15 minutes. Add the tomatoes, thyme, nutmeg, cinnamon, and cloves, season with salt and pepper, and stir to combine. Bring to a boil, reduce the heat to low, cover, and cook, while stirring every 30 minutes or so, for 2 hours. If the sauce looks too watery after 1½ hours of cooking, let it cook uncovered for the last 30 minutes. Discard the thyme sprigs and let cool.

2 Prepare the white sauce. Melt the butter in a medium saucepan over medium heat. Add the flour and whisk until a paste forms. Cook until the roux turns a pale shade of caramel, 6 to 8 minutes. Pour in the milk, very slowly at first (if you add it too fast, the roux will become lumpy) while whisking until all the milk has been added. Bring the sauce to a boil over medium heat and whisk until the sauce thickens. Remove from heat and let cool for 10 to 15 minutes. Stir in the nutmeg, salt, and cheese and then slowly add 1 ladleful of the white sauce to the eggs while whisking vigorously. Add another ladleful while continuing to whisk. Add the tempered eggs to the white sauce and whisk until well combined. Lay a piece of plastic wrap directly on the surface of the sauce to keep a skin from forming.

3 Preheat the oven to 400°F. Grease the bottom and sides of a 9 x 13-inch baking dish with the butter. Bring a large pot of

INGREDIENTS

For the Meat Sauce

2 tablespoons extra virgin olive oil

2 onions, minced

Salt and black pepper, to taste

4 large garlic cloves,
peeled and minced

2 pounds ground lamb

2 cups whole milk

1 (28 oz.) can of tomato puree

4 sprigs of fresh thyme

1½ teaspoons nutmeg, grated

1 teaspoon ground cinnamon

10 whole cloves

For the White Sauce

8 tablespoons (1 stick) unsalted butter

½ cup all-purpose flour,
plus 2 tablespoons

4 cups whole milk

1½ teaspoons nutmeg, grated

1½ teaspoons salt

1⅓ cups Parmesan cheese, grated

3 large egg yolks, beaten

For the Pastitsio

1½ tablespoons unsalted butter

1 pound ziti

1 cup panko bread crumbs

⅓ cup Parmesan cheese, grated

water to a boil. Once it's boiling, add salt (1 tablespoon for every 4 cups water) and stir. Add the ziti and cook the pasta for ³/₄ of the directed time. Drain, transfer to the prepared baking dish along with 2 cups of the white sauce, and toss to coat. Once cool enough to handle, arrange the ziti so that they are all lined up side by side. Spread the remaining white sauce over the top.

4 Reduce the oven temperature to 375°F. Place the dish in the oven and bake until the sauce is bubbling, 40 to 45 minutes. While the dish is baking, reheat the meat sauce. Toss the bread crumbs and Parmesan together in a medium bowl. Remove the dish from the oven and sprinkle the bread crumb-and-cheese mixture evenly over the top. Return to the oven and turn on the broiler. Remove the dish when the crumb topping turns golden brown and let cool for 15 minutes before slicing. Ladle the meat sauce into the bottom of a warm bowl and then top with a slice of the Pastitsio.

Baked Rigatoni with Mushrooms, Leeks, and Sausage

**YIELD: 6 TO 8 SERVINGS • ACTIVE TIME: 1½ HOURS
TOTAL TIME: 2½ HOURS**

The only possible way to make this rustic rigatoni dish even more delicious would be to use fresh porcini mushrooms instead of cremini. Thankfully, the small amount of dried porcini required by the recipe adds a nice measure of that fungi's irresistible woodsy flavor.

1 Bring a large pot of water to a boil. Once it's boiling, add salt (1 tablespoon for every 4 cups) and stir. Add the pasta and cook for ¾ of the time instructed on the package. Drain, rinse under cold water, and drain again. Transfer to a bowl, add ½ tablespoon of the olive oil, stir to combine, and cover.

2 Place the porcini mushrooms in a small bowl with water and soak until they have softened, about 15 minutes. Lightly run your fingers across all the pieces to dislodge any dirt or debris. Gather them in your hand and gently squeeze over the bowl to remove excess water, then chop. Strain the soaking liquid through a paper towel-lined sieve and reserve 1½ cups. Set aside.

3 Place the leeks in a large bowl of water and swish them around to remove any dirt. Drain well, transfer to a kitchen towel, and set aside.

4 Heat a large skillet over medium-low for 2 to 3 minutes, then add 2 tablespoons each of the butter and oil. Once the butter has melted, add the leeks, season with salt, raise the heat to medium, and cook, while stirring occasionally, until the leeks are soft, about 15 minutes. Remove from heat, season with pepper, add the nutmeg, transfer to a bowl, and set aside.

5 Wipe out the skillet and place it over medium-low heat for 2 to 3 minutes, then add 2 tablespoons each of the butter and oil. Once the butter has melted, add the porcini mushrooms and a pinch of salt and cook for 1 minute, then add the cremini mushrooms. Raise the heat to medium-high and cook, while stirring occasionally, until the mushrooms begin to release their liquid, about 6 minutes. Cook until the liquid has evaporated.

6 While the mushrooms cook, heat a medium skillet over medium-low for 2 to 3 minutes, then add the remaining oil and raise the heat to medium-high. Once it begins to glisten, add the bratwurst. Cook until the meat begins to turn a caramel color. Transfer to a bowl and set aside.

7 Preheat the oven to 350°F. Transfer the mushrooms to a very large bowl and add the béchamel and the reserved soaking water. Stir to combine, season to taste, and then add the leeks, bratwurst, ¾ cup of the Parmesan, and the cooked pasta. Toss to coat evenly. Transfer the mixture to a 9 x 13-inch baking dish, sprinkle the remaining Parmesan on top, and bake until the dish is bubbling, about 20 minutes.

INGREDIENTS

Salt and black pepper, to taste

1 pound rigatoni

5½ tablespoons extra virgin olive oil

1 oz. dried porcini mushrooms

5 large leeks, white and light green parts only, trimmed, and thinly sliced

4 tablespoons unsalted butter

2 teaspoons nutmeg, grated

1 pound cremini mushrooms, stemmed and chopped

1 pound bratwurst sausage, casings removed

2½ cups Béchamel Sauce (see page 82)

1¼ cups Parmesan cheese, grated

Under 30 Minutes

During the workweek, it never feels like the day contains enough hours. By the time you've dealt with everything at your job, navigated the evening commute, and responded to everyone and everything, preparing a meal that is delicious and nutritious enough to be worth the effort can seem daunting. With the world's ever-increasing demands in mind, we've gathered a series of enchanting dishes that can be prepared in almost no time, meaning that you'll actually have a few moments to sit down, relax, and gather your energies for the next day.

Penne with Asparagus and Ricotta Sauce

YIELD: 4 SERVINGS • ACTIVE TIME: 12 MINUTES
TOTAL TIME: 25 MINUTES

The deliciousness of this dish comes from combining the earthy brightness of fresh, in-season asparagus with the comforting creaminess of ricotta.

INGREDIENTS

2 pounds thin asparagus, woody ends removed

6 tablespoons water

2 cups whole milk ricotta cheese

Zest of ½ lemon

1 tablespoon extra virgin olive oil

Salt, to taste

1 pound pasta

6 tablespoons unsalted butter

Parmesan cheese, grated, for garnish

1 Bring a large pot of water to a boil. Lay the asparagus in a shallow microwave-safe bowl, add 1 tablespoon of the water, cover the dish with plastic wrap, and leave a small section loose to allow steam to escape. Microwave for 2 minutes and quickly transfer the asparagus to a large bowl filled with ice water. Cut off the asparagus tips and set them aside. Halve the remainder of the cooked spears, place them in a food processor with the remaining water, and puree until smooth.

2 In a small microwave-safe bowl, combine the ricotta, lemon zest, olive oil, and a couple pinches of salt.

3 When the water for the pasta is boiling, add salt (1 tablespoon for every 4 cups water) and stir. Add the pasta and cook 2 minutes less than the directed cooking time. Reserve ¼ cup of the pasta water and drain.

4 While the pasta cooks, heat a medium skillet over medium heat for 2 to 3 minutes. Add 2 tablespoons of the butter and raise the heat to medium-high. Once it's melted, add the asparagus tips and a couple pinches of salt. Cook, while stirring occasionally, until they develop a toasted color, about 2 minutes. Transfer them to a small warm bowl, leaving as much of the butter as possible behind in the skillet, and loosely cover the bowl with aluminum foil. Add another 3 tablespoons of butter to the skillet. Once it's melted, add the asparagus puree, season with salt, and cook, while stirring occasionally, until the puree starts gently bubbling, about 3 minutes. Reduce the heat to low and cover.

5 When the pasta is just about ready, place the bowl with the ricotta mixture in the microwave and heat for 1 minute. Stir thoroughly. Place the large pot over high heat, add the remaining butter, reserved pasta water, and the pasta. Toss until the water has been absorbed, add the asparagus puree and cook, while stirring, for 1 to 2 minutes. Divide the pasta between four warm bowls and top each one with ½ cup of the warm ricotta mixture, the asparagus tips, and Parmesan.

Orecchiette with Pancetta and Broccoli Rabe

YIELD: 4 SERVINGS • ACTIVE TIME: 15 MINUTES
TOTAL TIME: 25 MINUTES

The star of this quick and easy dish is the pancetta, which adds a savory unctuousness that will linger in the mind.

INGREDIENTS

3 pounds broccoli rabe

⅓ cup extra virgin olive oil, plus 2 tablespoons

3 garlic cloves, peeled

6 oz. pancetta, diced

1 teaspoon red pepper flakes

Salt and black pepper, to taste

¾ pound orecchiette, homemade (see pages 34-35) or store-bought

½ cup pecorino Romano cheese, grated, plus more for garnish

1 Bring a large pot of water to a boil. Fill a large bowl with cold water. Immerse the broccoli rabe in the bowl and swish it about to dislodge any dirt. Remove from the bowl and shake off the excess water. Using a sharp knife, trim off the thick stems and any discolored leaves. Slice across into ½-inch-wide strips.

2 Heat a small skillet over low heat for 2 to 3 minutes. Add the ⅓ cup of the oil and turn the heat up to medium. Add the garlic, pancetta, and red pepper flakes. Cook for 3 to 4 minutes, while stirring frequently, until the pancetta and garlic both turn lightly golden. Remove from heat, discard the garlic, and set the pan aside.

3 Once the pot of water is boiling, add salt (1 tablespoon for every 4 cups water) and stir. Add the broccoli rabe and pasta and cook 2 minutes less than the pasta's directed cooking time. Reserve ½ cup of the cooking water, drain, return the empty pot to the stove, and raise the heat to high. Add the remaining oil and reserved pasta water and stir. Add the drained broccoli rabe and pasta and toss until the water is absorbed. Add the contents of the skillet, season with pepper, and add the pecorino.

Cook, while tossing, for 2 minutes. Divide between four warm bowls and garnish with additional pecorino.

TIP: FOR BEST RESULTS, USE DAY-OLD BREAD THAT IS NOT ROCK HARD, AND CONSIDER USING SALT-PACKED ANCHOVIES.

Pici with Anchovy Bread Crumbs

**YIELD: 4 SERVINGS • ACTIVE TIME: 10 MINUTES
TOTAL TIME: 25 MINUTES**

Popular throughout Southern Italy, this anchovy-filled pasta dish is a remnant from a time when the working poor often had little more than stale bread and a few anchovies to subsist on.

1 Put a large pot of water on to boil for the pasta. Heat a heavy-bottomed skillet over medium heat for 2 to 3 minutes. Add the ⅓ cup of the olive oil and heat for a minute or 2. Add the anchovy fillets, mash them with a fork, and cook until they disintegrate, about 2 to 3 minutes. Raise the heat to medium-high and add the bread crumbs. Cook, while stirring often, until they are golden brown, about 2 to 3 minutes. Remove the skillet from heat, season with salt and pepper, and tent loosely with aluminum foil. Don't use a lid because it will create steam and make the bread crumbs mushy.

2 Once the pasta water is boiling, add salt (1 tablespoon for every 4 cups water) and stir. Add the pasta and cook 2 minutes less than the pasta's directed cooking time. Reserve ½ cup of the cooking water, drain, return the empty pot to the stove, and raise the heat to high. Add the remaining oil and reserved pasta water, and stir. Add the drained pasta and cook, while tossing continuously, for 2 minutes. Transfer the pasta to a warm serving bowl. Top with the warm anchovy-and-breadcrumb mixture and toss to combine. Garnish with the parsley before serving.

INGREDIENTS

⅓ cup extra virgin olive oil, plus 2½ tablespoons

10 anchovy fillets

2 cups bread crumbs

Salt and black pepper, to taste

¾ pound pici

2 handfuls of parsley, chopped, for garnish

Pici with Pecorino Cheese and Pepper

YIELD: 4 SERVINGS • ACTIVE TIME: 10 MINUTES
TOTAL TIME: 15 MINUTES

Essentially, this is high-end, Italian macaroni and cheese. Few dishes showcase the rewards of pan sauce precision like the rich, creamy, and slightly piquant result featured here.

INGREDIENTS

7 tablespoons extra virgin olive oil

2½ teaspoons black pepper

Salt, to taste

¾ pound pici

1 cup Parmesan cheese, grated, plus more for garnish

½ cup pecorino Sardo cheese, grated

1 Heat a large skillet over medium heat for 2 to 3 minutes. Add the olive oil and raise the heat to medium-high. When the oil is glistening, add the pepper and cook for 2 minutes. Remove the skillet from heat.

2 Bring a large pot of water to a boil. Once it is boiling, add salt (1 tablespoon for every 4 cups water) and stir. Add the pasta and cook 2 minutes less than the pasta's directed cooking time. Reserve ½ cup of the cooking water and use tongs to transfer the pici to the skillet. Raise the heat to high and toss to coat. Add the cheeses and 3 tablespoons of the pasta water and continue to toss until the pasta is coated. Add another tablespoon or 2 of pasta water if the dish seems too dry. Divide between four warm bowls, season with salt and pepper, and garnish with additional Parmesan.

Pici with Cherry Tomato, Tuna, and Caper Sauce

**YIELD: 4 SERVINGS • ACTIVE TIME: 10 MINUTES
TOTAL TIME: 25 MINUTES**

Zesty and fragrant, this olive oil-based sauce comes from the volcanic Lipari Islands north of Sicily, where both tuna and capers are plentiful.

INGREDIENTS

1 pint cherry tomatoes, chopped

3 tablespoons nonpareil capers, rinsed, drained, and minced

3 small garlic cloves, minced

Salt and black pepper, to taste

¾ pound pici

⅔ cup extra virgin olive oil, plus 1 teaspoon

1 (17 oz.) jar of olive oil-packed tuna, drained and crumbled

Handful of parsley, chopped, for garnish

1 Combine the tomatoes, capers, and garlic in a bowl and set aside. Bring a large pot of water to a boil. Once it is boiling, add salt (1 tablespoon for every 4 cups water) and stir. Add the pasta and cook 2 minutes less than the pasta's directed cooking time. Reserve ½ cup of the cooking water and then drain the pasta.

2 While the pasta water is heating up, start the sauce. Heat a large, deep skillet over medium heat for 2 to 3 minutes, add the ⅔ cup of the olive oil, and let it warm for a couple of minutes. Add the tomato mixture and cook for 3 to 4 minutes. Add the tuna, season generously with pepper, and stir to combine. Cook for another 5 minutes, remove the skillet from heat, and cover.

3 Return the large pot to the stove. Raise the heat to high and add the remaining oil and the reserved pasta water. Add the drained pasta and toss. Add the tuna-and-tomato mixture and cook, while tossing, for 2 minutes. Divide between four warm bowls and garnish with the parsley.

VARIATION: IF YOU'RE AFTER A MORE SAVORY PREPARATION, SWITCH OUT THE CHERRY TOMATOES FOR 1 CUP OF OLIVES.

INGREDIENTS

3 tablespoons
pine nuts

Salt and white pepper,
to taste

½ cup walnut pieces

2 black garlic cloves

½ cup mascarpone

3½ tablespoons
whole milk

3 tablespoons
Parmesan cheese,
grated

¾ pound
angel hair pasta

3 tablespoons
unsalted butter

Angel Hair with Walnut, Black Garlic, and Mascarpone Sauce

**YIELD: 4 SERVINGS • ACTIVE TIME: 10 MINUTES
TOTAL TIME: 15 MINUTES**

The rich, earthy-tasting sauce features black garlic, an ingredient that was developed in Korea and is quickly becoming a favorite of chefs in the United States. You can find it online, as well as at Trader Joe's and Whole Foods.

1 Bring a large pot of water to a boil. While the water comes to a boil, heat a small skillet over medium-low heat for 2 minutes. Add the pine nuts and cook, while stirring frequently, for 3 to 4 minutes. Remove from the heat, season with a pinch of salt, and set aside.

2 Place the walnuts and black garlic in a food processor and pulse until coarsely chopped. Transfer the mixture to a small saucepan and add the mascarpone, milk, and Parmesan. Season with salt and pepper and cook the mixture over medium-low heat until just before it starts to boil. Remove from heat and cover.

3 Once the pasta water is boiling, add salt (1 tablespoon for every 4 cups water) and stir. Add the pasta and cook 2 minutes less than the pasta's directed cooking time. Reserve ¼ cup of the cooking water, drain, return the empty pot to the stove, and raise the heat to high. Add the butter and reserved pasta water and stir. Add the drained pasta and cook, while tossing continuously, for 2 minutes. Add the contents of the small saucepan and cook, while tossing, for 1 to 2 minutes. Divide the pasta between four warm bowls and top with the pine nuts.

Fettuccine with Pancetta, Hazelnuts, Orange, and Sage

YIELD: 4 SERVINGS • ACTIVE TIME: 10 MINUTES
TOTAL TIME: 25 MINUTES

The unlikely duo of hazelnuts and pancetta meld well in this dish, particularly when joined by the tart brightness of citrus and the piney aroma of sage.

1 Bring the wine to a gentle boil in a small saucepan and continue to boil until reduced by half, about 5 minutes. Remove from heat and let cool slightly.

2 Heat a large skillet over low heat for 2 to 3 minutes. Add 2 tablespoons of the olive oil and raise the heat to medium. Once the oil begins to glisten, add the pancetta and cook, while stirring occasionally, until it turns golden brown, about 8 minutes. Add the hazelnuts and toast for 2 to 3 minutes while stirring. Transfer the pancetta and hazelnuts to a small bowl. Raise the heat to medium and wait a minute. Add the reduced wine and cook for 5 minutes. Add the butter, sage leaves, and orange zest and bring to a gentle boil. Remove from the heat and cover to keep warm. Bring a large pot of water to a boil. Once it's boiling, add salt (1 tablespoon for every 4 cups water) and stir. Add the pasta and cook for 2 minutes less than the directed cooking time. Drain the pasta and return the empty pot to the stove. Immediately turn the heat to high, add the remaining oil and the broth, and stir.

INGREDIENTS

1 cup dry white wine

3 tablespoons extra virgin olive oil

4 thick-cut slices of pancetta, diced

½ cup blanched hazelnuts, chopped

4 tablespoons unsalted butter, chilled

5 to 7 sage leaves

Zest of ½ orange

Salt and black pepper, to taste

¾ pound fettuccine

¾ cup chicken broth, very hot

3 Add the drained pasta and toss until the broth is absorbed. Add the pancetta-and-hazelnut mixture and cook, tossing continuously, for 2 minutes. Season with salt and pepper and then divide the pasta between four warm bowls.

TIP: REGULAR BACON DOES NOT MAKE A GOOD SUBSTITUTE FOR THE PANCETTA IN THIS RECIPE BECAUSE ITS SMOKINESS OVERSHADOWS THE TOFFEE-LIKE TASTE OF THE HAZELNUTS.

Fettuccine Alfredo

YIELD: 4 SERVINGS • ACTIVE TIME: 15 MINUTES
TOTAL TIME: 20 MINUTES

Despite originating in Italy, fettuccine alfredo is much more popular in the United States. This recipe stays faithful to the dish's origins, switching out all that heavy cream for an emulsion of melted butter, grated cheese, and starchy pasta water.

1 Cut 4 tablespoons of the butter into 4 pieces and set aside. Bring a large pot of water to a boil. Once it's boiling, add salt (1 tablespoon for every 4 cups water) and stir. Add the fettuccine and cook for 2 minutes less than the directed cooking time. Reserve ½ cup of the pasta water, drain the pasta, and set aside.

2 While the pasta is cooking, transfer 1 cup of pasta water to a large skillet. Bring to a gentle simmer over medium heat and then whisk in the 4 tablespoons of butter, one piece at a time, until emulsified. Add the Parmesan gradually while whisking constantly, making sure what you've added is completely melted and incorporated into the sauce before adding more.

3 Return the large pot to the stove and turn the heat to high. Add the remaining butter and ½ of the reserved pasta water. Add the drained pasta and toss until the liquid has been absorbed. Transfer the pasta to the skillet and toss to coat, adding more pasta water as needed. Divide the pasta between four warm bowls, season with salt and pepper, and garnish with additional Parmesan.

INGREDIENTS

4½ tablespoons unsalted butter

Salt and black pepper, to taste

¾ pound fettuccine

1 cup Parmesan cheese, grated, plus more for garnish

Fettuccine with Madeira Cream Sauce and Pancetta

**YIELD: 4 SERVINGS • ACTIVE TIME: 10 MINUTES
TOTAL TIME: 30 MINUTES**

The hodgepodge of ingredients may seem like an insurmountable obstacle, but this lightly creamy and remarkably fragrant dish comes together magically.

INGREDIENTS

1 cup Madeira wine

4 sage leaves

1 sprig of rosemary

1 tablespoon extra virgin olive oil

4 oz. pancetta, chopped

2½ tablespoons unsalted butter

1 small Vidalia onion, chopped

Salt and freshly ground white pepper, to taste

¾ pound fettuccine

½ cup heavy cream

Manchego cheese, grated, for garnish

1 Bring the Madeira to a boil in a small saucepan and continue to boil until reduced almost by half. Remove from heat and set aside.

2 Set 3 of sage leaves aside and slice the fourth one very thin. Set aside. Remove ⅓ of the leaves from the sprig of rosemary and mince. Leave the rest of the rosemary sprig as is and set aside.

3 Heat a large skillet over medium-low heat for 2 to 3 minutes. Add the olive oil and increase the heat to medium. Once the oil begins to glisten, add the pancetta and cook, while stirring occasionally, until it renders its fat and turns a golden caramel color, about 8 minutes. Transfer the pancetta to a small bowl. Add 2 tablespoons of the butter to the skillet and raise the heat to medium-high. Once it melts, add the onion and season with salt and pepper. Add the 3 sage leaves and the rosemary sprig and stir. When the onion starts to sizzle, reduce the heat to low, cover, and cook, while stirring occasionally, until very soft, about 20 minutes.

4 While the onion cooks, put a large pot of water on to boil for the pasta. Once it's boiling, add salt (1 tablespoon for every 4 cups water) and stir. Add the pasta and cook for 2 minutes less than the directed cooking time. Reserve ¼ cup of the pasta water and drain the pasta.

5 When the onion is cooked and you've added the pasta to the water, remove the sage leaves and rosemary sprig from the onion mixture. Raise the heat to

medium-high under the skillet and add the cream and reduced Madeira. Cook, while stirring occasionally, until the sauce thickens, about 8 minutes.

6 Return the large pot to the stove, raise the heat to high, and add the remaining butter and the reserved pasta water. Add the drained pasta and toss. Add the onion mixture and cook, while tossing continuously, for 2 minutes. Divide the pasta between four warm bowls and top with the pancetta, the thinly sliced sage, the rosemary, and the Manchego.

Spaghetti with Mussels, Parsley, and Garlic

YIELD: 4 SERVINGS • ACTIVE TIME: 10 MINUTES
TOTAL TIME: 25 MINUTES

This is a riff on *zuppa de' peoci*, which is a traditional Venetian soup. In this version the bread is replaced by spaghetti, but you may want to keep a few slices around to dip in what remains of the delicious sauce.

INGREDIENTS

½ cup dry white wine

2 cups water

2 pounds mussels, scrubbed and debearded

¼ cup extra virgin olive oil, plus 1 teaspoon

3 garlic cloves, peeled and thinly sliced

3 very ripe plum tomatoes, concasse (see page 50) and chopped

Salt and black pepper, to taste

2 handfuls of parsley, chopped

¾ pound spaghetti

1 Bring the wine to a boil in a small saucepan and continue to boil until reduced almost by half. Remove from heat and set aside.

2 Bring the water to a boil in a large pot. Place the mussels in the pot, cover, and reduce the heat to medium. They will quickly begin to open with the heat. As they do, pluck them out with kitchen tongs and transfer to a large bowl. When most of the mussels have all opened, discard the few that remain closed, strain the cooking liquid through a paper towel-lined fine sieve, and reserve it. Set mussels and strained liquid aside.

3 Put a large pot of water on to boil for the pasta. Heat a large skillet over medium-low heat for 2 to 3 minutes. Add the ¼ cup of the olive oil and warm for a couple of minutes. Add the garlic, tomatoes, and a couple generous pinches of salt, raise the heat to medium-high, and cook for 5 minutes, while stirring a few times. Season with pepper and stir in the parsley. Add the mussels, the reserved cooking liquid, and the reduced wine, cover, and cook until the liquid on the bottom of the pot starts boiling, about 8 minutes.

4 When the pasta water is boiling, add salt (1 tablespoon for every 4 cups water) and stir. Add the pasta and cook for 2 minutes less than the directed cooking time. Reserve ¼ cup of the pasta water, drain the pasta, and return the pot to the stove. Raise the heat to high, add the remaining oil and the reserved pasta water. Add the drained pasta and toss. Add the contents of the skillet and cook, while tossing continuously, for 2 minutes. Divide the pasta between four warm bowls.

Classic Buttered Noodles with Parmesan

**YIELD: 4 SERVINGS • ACTIVE TIME: 10 MINUTES
TOTAL TIME: 20 MINUTES**

Known as "Pini pasta" in some circles, this simple, speedy, and tasty dish reminds some of childhood. Though it's so satisfying that no one ever really outgrows it.

INGREDIENTS

Salt and white pepper, to taste

¾ pound flat egg noodles

5½ tablespoons unsalted butter at room temperature

½ cup Parmesan cheese, grated, plus more for garnish

Handful of parsley, chopped

1 Bring a large pot of water to a boil. Once it's boiling, add salt (1 tablespoon for every 4 cups water) and stir. Add the noodles and cook for 2 minutes less than the directed cooking time. Reserve ¼ cup of the pasta water, drain the pasta, and return the pot to the stove. Immediately raise the heat to high, add ½ tablespoon of the butter and the reserved pasta water. Add the drained pasta and toss.

2 Add the remaining butter, the Parmesan, and parsley, season with salt and pepper, and cook, while tossing continuously, for 2 minutes. Transfer to a large bowl, sprinkle with additional Parmesan, and serve.

Tagliatelle with Creamy Lemon Sauce

YIELD: 4 SERVINGS • ACTIVE TIME: 10 MINUTES
TOTAL TIME: 25 MINUTES

Ideal for hot summer days, this refreshing pasta dish makes you feel as though you're having a lovely meal in Sorrento, the enchanting town on the Amalfi Coast.

1 Put a large pot of water on to boil for the pasta. Put the lemon zest and juice in a 2-cup measuring cup along with 4 tablespoons of the butter, the cream, pepper, and a few generous pinches of salt. Put the measuring cup in a microwave and heat on high for 45 to 60 seconds, until the butter is fully melted. Cover and set aside.

2 When the pasta water is boiling, add salt (1 tablespoon for every 4 cups water) and stir. Add the pasta and cook for 2 minutes less than the directed cooking time. Reserve ¼ cup of the pasta water, drain the pasta, and return the empty pot to the stove. Immediately turn the heat to high and add the remaining butter and the reserved pasta water. Add the drained pasta and toss. Add the warm lemon-and-cream mixture and the Parmesan and cook, while tossing continuously, for 2 minutes. Divide the pasta between four warm bowls and garnish with additional Parmesan.

INGREDIENTS

Zest and juice of 1 lemon

5 tablespoons unsalted butter, cut into small pieces

½ cup heavy cream, plus more as needed

¼ teaspoon freshly ground white pepper

Salt, to taste

¾ pound tagliatelle

½ cup Parmesan cheese, grated, plus more for garnish

Tagliatelle with Gorgonzola Cream Sauce and Pan-Toasted Spiced Walnuts

**YIELD: 4 SERVINGS • ACTIVE TIME: 12 MINUTES
TOTAL TIME: 25 MINUTES**

Those who find Gorgonzola a bit too biting will reconsider after tasting this cream sauce. The key is using Gorgonzola dolce, a variety that is aged less than regular Gorgonzola, giving it a milder flavor.

1 Heat a large nonstick skillet over low heat for a minute. Add the olive oil and steak seasoning, stir, and raise the heat to medium. Once the oil begins to sizzle, stir for 30 seconds, then add the honey and water and stir again. Add the walnuts and toss to coat. Sprinkle them with the sugar, a pinch of salt, and the cayenne and cook, while stirring frequently, until the walnuts are lightly browned, 2 to 3 minutes. Transfer to a parchment paper-lined baking sheet so they are in a single layer and let cool completely.

2 While the nuts cool, bring a large pot of water to a boil. When the water is boiling, add salt (1 tablespoon for every 4 cups water) and stir. Add the pasta and cook for 2 minutes less than the directed cooking time. Reserve ¼ cup of the pasta water, drain the pasta, and set aside.

3 While the pasta is cooking, heat the cream and cheeses together in a medium saucepan over medium heat until the mixture is gently simmering. Continue to simmer the sauce until it is thick enough to coat the back of a spoon, about 8 minutes. Season with the nutmeg, salt, and pepper.

4 Return the large pot to the stove. Immediately turn the heat to high and add the butter and reserved pasta water. Add the pasta and toss until the water is absorbed. Add the sauce and cook, while stirring, for 1 to 2 minutes. Ladle the pasta into four warm bowls and top with the walnuts.

INGREDIENTS

1 tablespoon olive oil

1 teaspoon
steak seasoning

1 tablespoon honey

½ tablespoon water

1 cup walnut halves

1 tablespoon sugar

Salt and white pepper,
to taste

⅛ teaspoon cayenne
pepper

¾ pound tagliatelle

2 cups heavy cream

4 oz. Gorgonzola
dolce cheese,
chopped

⅔ cup Parmesan
cheese, grated, plus
more for garnish

1 teaspoon nutmeg,
grated

½ tablespoon
unsalted butter

TIP: IF YOU PREFER A PASTA
OTHER THAN TAGLIATELLE,
PENNE WORKS WELL IN THIS
PARTICULAR PREPARATION.

Vegetable & Other Alternative Noodles

As we learn more and more about nutrition, people are increasingly altering their diet to give themselves an edge. And while noodles are grand, the considerable carbohydrates and gluten many of them contain has removed them from many people's radar. If you, or someone you love, are one of these folks, we have a series of vegetable and alternative noodles that will scratch that itch without forcing anyone to deviate from their quest for self-improvement. These noodles are also good options if you're looking for a light, inventive, and aesthetically pleasing side to pair with a heavier main course.

INGREDIENTS

2 teaspoons
sesame seeds

2 tablespoons
smooth peanut butter

2 tablespoons water

2 tablespoons
seasoned rice vinegar

1 tablespoon soy sauce

1 tablespoon light
brown sugar

2 teaspoons toasted
sesame oil

1 teaspoon
chili bean sauce

1-inch piece of ginger,
peeled and grated

2 tablespoons peanut
oil, plus more as
needed

4 to 6 very large carrots,
peeled and either
spiralized or
grated thick

Salt, to taste

Scallions, chopped,
for garnish

Sesame Stir-Fried Carrot Noodles

YIELD: 4 SERVINGS • ACTIVE TIME: 30 MINUTES
TOTAL TIME: 30 MINUTES

As tasty as it is beautiful, this stir-fry benefits greatly from the spiciness of the ginger and the sweetness of the carrots.

Put the sesame seeds in a small skillet over medium heat and toast until golden brown and aromatic, about 8 minutes. Transfer them to a small bowl and set aside.

Whisk the peanut butter, water, vinegar, soy sauce, sugar, sesame oil, chili bean sauce, and ginger together in a small saucepan and cook over medium-low heat. Bring to a gentle boil and cook, while stirring frequently, until the sauce thickens, 4 to 5 minutes. Set aside.

Heat a wok or a large skillet over medium heat for 2 to 3 minutes. Raise the heat to medium-high and add the peanut oil. When the oil begins to glisten, add half of the carrots and a pinch of salt, and stir-fry until the carrots have softened, about 2 minutes. Transfer the carrots to a bowl and set aside. Repeat the process, adding a drizzle of peanut oil if necessary, with the remaining carrots. Add the peanut butter mixture to the bowl and toss with the carrots until they are evenly coated with it. Top with the sesame seeds and scallions and serve.

Cucumber Noodles with Coconut, Lime, and Cumin Dressing

YIELD: 4 SERVINGS • ACTIVE TIME: 30 MINUTES
TOTAL TIME: 45 MINUTES

A refreshing and spicy cucumber salad that is perfect for the summer, as it's fairly easy to assemble and the combination of cumin and coconut is endlessly satisfying.

INGREDIENTS

5 large cucumbers, peeled, halved, and seeded

1 cup unsweetened coconut, shredded

¼ cup coconut water

Zest and juice from 2 limes

1 teaspoon chili-garlic sauce

1 teaspoon ginger, grated

1 teaspoon sugar

1 teaspoon cumin

1 teaspoon salt

Scallions, thinly sliced, for garnish

½ cup salted, roasted peanuts, chopped, for garnish

1 Cut each cucumber half into as many ⅛-inch slices as possible. Then cut the slices into noodles that are ⅛-inch wide. Place the cucumber strands on paper towels to drain.

2 Place the coconut, coconut water, lime juice, chili-garlic sauce, ginger, sugar, cumin, and salt in a small food processor or a blender and puree until smooth. Transfer the cucumber noodles to a large serving bowl. Top with the sauce and toss to coat. Chill for at least 15 minutes and up to 2 hours in the refrigerator. Sprinkle with lime zest, scallions, and peanuts and serve.

Spaghetti Squash Noodles with Toasted Spiced Pecans

YIELD: 4 SERVINGS • ACTIVE TIME: 30 MINUTES
TOTAL TIME: 1 HOUR AND 15 MINUTES

This is the perfect offering when vegan or vegetarian friends and family come to visit, or when you are in the mood to eat something delicious, wholesome, and sustaining.

1 Preheat the oven to 400°F. Line a large baking pan with parchment paper. Cut each squash into four medallions and set them in the prepared pan. Place in the oven and bake until the strands are tender but still firm, 50 to 60 minutes. Remove from the oven and let cool for 10 minutes. Using a fork, pull the strands into the center of each round. Working in two batches, transfer half of the strands to a kitchen towel and gently squeeze to remove as much water as possible. Transfer the squash to a large bowl and repeat this step with the rest of the squash. Set aside.

2 Squeeze the blanched chard to remove as much liquid as possible and then mince. Place the pecans in a small plastic bag and gently crush them with a rolling pin. Heat a skillet for 2 to 3 minutes over low heat. Add 2 teaspoons of the olive oil, the chili powder, and sugar and cook. Once the mixture starts to gently sizzle, add the pecans and stir until coated. Continue to cook and stir until you begin to smell the nuts give off a toasty fragrance, about 2 minutes. Season with salt, stir, and transfer to a plate.

3 Heat a large skillet over low heat for 2 to 3 minutes. Add 1 tablespoon of the oil and heat for a minute or 2, then add the garlic, red pepper flakes, rosemary, and a pinch of salt. Cook until the garlic just starts to turn golden, 2 to 3 minutes. Raise the heat to medium-high, add the

INGREDIENTS

4 pounds spaghetti squash, ends trimmed and seeded

1 pound Swiss chard, stemmed and blanched

½ cup pecans

3 tablespoons extra virgin olive oil, plus 2 teaspoons

1 teaspoon chili powder

1 teaspoon sugar

Salt and white pepper, to taste

2 garlic cloves, minced

½ teaspoon red pepper flakes

1 sprig of rosemary, leaves minced

1 teaspoon Chinese black vinegar

¾ cup Parmesan cheese, grated

chard and a pinch of salt, stir to combine, and cook for 3 minutes. Transfer the chard to a warm bowl and tent with foil to keep warm. Add the remaining olive oil and let it heat for 1 to 2 minutes. Add the spaghetti squash strands, season with salt, and toss to coat. Sprinkle the vinegar over the top, season with salt and pepper, and toss again. Remove from the heat, add the Parmesan, and toss to coat. Divide between four warm bowls and top with the pecans.

Baked Spaghetti Squash with Tomato Sauce, Béchamel, and Ricotta

YIELD: 4 TO 6 SERVINGS • ACTIVE TIME: 40 MINUTES
TOTAL TIME: 1 HOUR AND 45 MINUTES

The key to this dish is removing as much of the moisture from the spaghetti squash as possible, since too much can drown all the wonderful flavors of this simple, tasty preparation.

INGREDIENTS

Preheat the oven to 400°F. Line a large baking pan with parchment paper. Cut each squash into four medallions and set them in the prepared pan. Place in the oven and bake until the strands are tender but still firm, 50 to 60 minutes. Remove from the oven and let cool for 10 minutes. Using a fork, pull the strands into the center of each round. Working in two batches, transfer half of the strands to a kitchen towel and gently squeeze to remove as much water as possible. Transfer the squash to a large bowl and repeat this step with the rest of the squash. Set aside.

Preheat the oven to 375°F. When ready to bake, add the salt, tomato sauce, and béchamel to the strands of squash and mix gently but thoroughly. Butter a 9 x 5-inch baking dish and transfer the squash mixture to it. Place in the oven and bake until bubbly and heated through, about 25 minutes. Remove from the oven and dot the top with the ricotta. Turn on the broiler and place an oven rack at the top level. Return the dish to the oven and broil until dark caramel-colored spots develop on the ricotta and squash, 2 to 3 minutes. Garnish with the basil and serve.

Egg Fettuccine with Gingery Red Pepper Sauce and Leeks

**YIELD: 4 SERVINGS • ACTIVE TIME: 30 MINUTES
TOTAL TIME: 45 MINUTES**

Seasoned with chives, cilantro, soy sauce, and sherry, eggs are easily disguised as hearty and flavorful fettuccine noodles. Top with a sprinkling of cilantro to complement the wonderful array of tastes present in this dish.

1 Place the leeks in a large bowl of water and swish them around to remove any dirt. Drain well, transfer to a kitchen towel, and set aside.

2 Heat a large skillet over medium-low heat for 2 to 3 minutes. Add the oils and raise the heat to medium. When the oil is glistening, add the leeks and a couple pinches of salt and stir. When the leeks start to sizzle, reduce the heat to low, cover, and cook, while stirring occasionally, until very soft and browned in spots, about 20 minutes. Remove from heat, let cool slightly, and strain through a fine sieve.

3 Whisk the eggs, cooked leeks, chives, cilantro, soy sauce, sherry, and a couple pinches of salt together in a medium bowl. Heat the skillet that contained the leeks (don't wipe it out) over medium-high heat. If there is a film of oil over the bottom, you are set. If not, add a tablespoon of peanut oil. Pour enough of the egg mixture into the skillet so that it just covers the bottom, while swirling the skillet continuously. Cook until the egg sets. Gently slide it onto a large plate, flip it, and then slide it back into the skillet and cook another 20 to 30 seconds. Transfer to a parchment paper-covered surface. Repeat the process

INGREDIENTS

4 leeks, white and light green parts only, trimmed and thinly sliced

2 tablespoons peanut oil, plus more as needed

1 tablespoon toasted sesame oil

Salt, to taste

8 large eggs

¼ cup chives, thinly sliced

2 handfuls of cilantro, chopped, plus more for garnish

2 tablespoons soy sauce

2 tablespoons dry sherry

Gingery Red Pepper Sauce (see pages 188-189), warm

three more times with the rest of the egg mixture, adding a small bit of oil as needed. As you finish, you can pile the rounds of cooked egg on top of one another. When all of the egg mixture has been cooked, slice the stack into thin strips and then gently separate them into strands. Divide the egg strips between four warm bowls, top with the sauce and the cilantro, and serve.

TIP: THE ONLY TIME-CONSUMING ASPECT OF PREPARING THIS DISH IS WORKING IN TWO BATCHES IN ORDER TO PERFECTLY BROWN THE EGGPLANT STRANDS. USE TWO FRYING PANS FOR SPEEDIER RESULTS.

Hot and Garlicky Eggplant Noodles

YIELD: 4 SERVINGS • ACTIVE TIME: 45 MINUTES
TOTAL TIME: 45 MINUTES

The browned strands of eggplant fill two voids in this vegetarian dish, supplying meaty flavor and tender noodles in a dish that features neither.

INGREDIENTS

4 pounds eggplant, ends trimmed and peeled

2 tablespoons chili-garlic paste

2 teaspoons water

3 tablespoons extra virgin olive oil

1 tablespoon toasted sesame oil

Salt, to taste

2 handfuls of cilantro, thinly sliced, for garnish

½ cup tamari almonds, chopped, for garnish

1 Cut each eggplant into ¼-inch-thick slices, then cut each slice into ¼-inch-wide strips. Place the chili-garlic paste and water in a small bowl and stir until well combined.

2 You will need to work in batches to cook the eggplant. Heat a large nonstick frying pan over medium heat for 1 minute. Add half of the olive oil, sesame oil, and chili-garlic mixture and raise the heat to medium-high. When the oil begins to glisten, add half of the eggplant noodles and a couple pinches of salt. Cook, while stirring frequently, until the strands have softened and started turning a rich caramel color, about 5 minutes. Transfer to a warmed serving platter and tent loosely with aluminum foil. Wipe the pan with a paper towel and repeat the process using the remaining eggplant, olive oil, sesame oil, and chili-garlic mixture. Garnish with the cilantro and almonds and serve.

Eggplant Noodles with Chicken and Mixed Peppers

YIELD: 4 SERVINGS • ACTIVE TIME: 35 MINUTES
TOTAL TIME: 35 MINUTES

Shaoxing rice wine's legendary ability to enhance the meaty flavor in any dish is on full display here, as both the chicken and eggplant shine from its inclusion.

1 Cut each eggplant into ¼-inch-thick slices, then cut each slice into ¼-inch-wide strips. Place the chili-garlic paste and water in a small bowl and stir until well combined.

2 Whisk the rice wine (or sherry), soy sauce, and sesame oil together in a medium bowl. Add the chicken and toss until well coated.

3 Heat a large wok or skillet over medium-high heat for 2 to 3 minutes and add 2 tablespoons of the peanut oil. Once it begins to shimmer but is not yet smoking, add the chicken and marinade and stir-fry until cooked through, 3 to 4 minutes. Transfer to a warm plate. Add the remaining peanut oil. Let the oil heat for a minute or two, until it begins to swirl on the surface but is not yet smoking, then add the peppers and stir-fry until soft, about 3 minutes. Add the garlic and scallions and stir-fry until they soften and start turning slightly golden brown, about 2 minutes.

4 Return the chicken to the pan, add the eggplant noodles and stir-fry until everything's heated through, about 5 minutes.

INGREDIENTS

4 pounds eggplant, ends trimmed and peeled

2 tablespoons Shaoxing rice wine or dry sherry

1 tablespoon soy sauce

2 teaspoons toasted sesame oil

½ pound boneless, skinless chicken breast, sliced into thin strips

4 tablespoons peanut oil

2 jalapeño peppers, seeded and thinly sliced

1 red bell pepper, seeded and cut into thin strips

2 garlic cloves, peeled and thinly sliced

2 scallions, white and light green parts only, cut into 2-inch-long pieces

Zucchini Noodles with Oven-Roasted Stilton, Radicchio, and Peaches

YIELD: 4 SERVINGS • ACTIVE TIME: 30 MINUTES
TOTAL TIME: 45 MINUTES

When peaches are in season, you almost can't find enough uses for them. With this salad, you've got another outlet for their juicy sweetness.

Bring a large pot of water to a boil. Once it's boiling, add salt (1 tablespoon of salt for every 4 cups of water). Place the zucchini in the boiling salted water and cook for 2 minutes. Drain and run under cold water until cool. Drain again and set aside.

Place the pine nuts in a small skillet over medium heat and cook, while stirring continuously, for 4 to 5 minutes. Remove from the heat and let cool.

Preheat the oven to 500°F. Place the pine nuts, basil, and lemon juice in a food processor and puree until smooth. Transfer the mixture to a large bowl, add the olive oil, season with salt and pepper, and whisk for 1 minute. Add the blanched zucchini and toss to coat.

Place the cheese, lemon zest, honey, and a pinch of salt and pepper in a small bowl and toss gently. Transfer the cheese mixture to a parchment-lined baking sheet, put on the center rack of the oven, turn the broiler on, and broil until the top of the mixture turns golden, 2 to 3 minutes. Remove from the oven and let cool for 1 to 2 minutes. Arrange the shredded radicchio leaves on a platter and top with the zucchini, peach wedges, roasted Stilton, and cranberries. Serve at room temperature.

INGREDIENTS

Salt and black pepper, to taste

4 zucchini, ends trimmed, julienned

⅓ cup pine nuts

2 handfuls of basil, chopped

Zest and juice of 1 lemon

2 tablespoons extra virgin olive oil

4 oz. Stilton cheese, crumbled

1½ tablespoons honey

2 cups radicchio, shredded

1 ripe peach, halved, pitted, and cut into wedges

1 tablespoon dried cranberries

Squid Pasta with Garlic Sauce

**YIELD: 4 SERVINGS • ACTIVE TIME: 45 MINUTES
TOTAL TIME: 1 HOUR**

This gluten-free dish relies on the unmistakable flavor of shichimi togarashi, a Japanese seven-spice powder containing red pepper flakes, orange peel, sesame seeds, Sichuan pepper, ginger, poppy seeds, and seaweed.

1 Fill a small bowl with cold water and add the vinegar. Add the mushrooms and swirl them around in the water for 30 seconds or so. Transfer them to a colander and rinse under cold water. Drain well and place them on a kitchen towel with the stem end facing down. Let air-dry for 15 minutes, then thinly slice and set aside.

2 Sprinkle the squid with salt and pepper. Combine the mirin and soy sauce in a small bowl. Heat a large skillet over medium heat for 2 to 3 minutes and then add the butter. Once it melts, add the garlic and cook until it starts to sizzle. Raise the heat to medium-high, add the mushrooms, and cook for 1 minute. Add the squid strips and asparagus and season with salt and pepper. Cook until the squid strips turn opaque and begin curling, about 2 minutes. Drizzle the mirin mixture over everything and toss well to combine. Divide between four warmed plates and sprinkle with shichimi togarashi before serving.

INGREDIENTS

1 tablespoon distilled white vinegar

4 large shiitake mushrooms, stemmed

¾ pound squid, cleaned, scored, and cut into ½-inch strips

Salt and black pepper, to taste

5 tablespoons mirin

2 tablespoons tamari or soy sauce

3 tablespoons unsalted butter

3 garlic cloves, peeled and thinly sliced

16 thin asparagus spears, cut into 2-inch pieces on a diagonal

Shichimi togarashi (Japanese seven-spice powder), for dusting

Desserts

Noodles are almost exclusively utilized in savory preparations. But if we've learned anything through our love affair with them, it's to refrain from boxing them in. As it turns out, there is plenty of space for the ever-versatile noodle to provide the sweet ending so many of us crave at the conclusion of a meal.

You might still be skeptical, but after you try the Chocolate Fettuccine with Pears, Candied Ginger, and Gorgonzola Cheese (see pages 254–255) or the Portuguese Vermicelli Pudding (see pages 262–263), we're pretty confident you'll start to see things our way.

Chocolate Pasta Dough

YIELD: 1¼ POUNDS • ACTIVE TIME: 1 HOUR
TOTAL TIME: 1½ HOURS

Do not be concerned about the amount of cocoa powder in this recipe, as the resulting dark brown pasta tastes delightfully of chocolate but contains no hint of bitterness.

INGREDIENTS

1½ cups all-purpose flour, plus more as needed

½ cup unsweetened cocoa powder, plus more for dusting

3 large eggs

1 tablespoon water, plus more as needed

1 tablespoon extra virgin olive oil

1 On a flat work surface, combine the flour and cocoa and form it into a mound. Create a well in the center, then add the eggs, water, and olive oil. Using a fork or your fingertips, gradually start pulling the flour mixture into the pool of egg, beginning with the inner rim of the well. Continue to gradually add flour until the dough starts holding together in a single mass, adding more water—1 tablespoon at a time—if the mixture is too dry to stick together. Once the dough feels firm and dry, and can form a craggy-looking ball, it's time to start kneading.

2 Begin by working the remaining flour on the work surface into the ball of dough. Using the heel of your hand, push the ball of dough away from you in a downward motion. Turn the dough 45 degrees each time you repeat this motion, as doing so incorporates the flour more evenly. Eventually, the dough will have a smooth, elastic texture. If the dough still feels wet, tacky,

or sticky, dust it with flour and continue kneading. If it feels too dry and is not completely sticking together, wet your hands with water and continue kneading. Wet your hands as many times as you need in order to help the flour shape into a ball. Knead for 8 to 10 minutes. The dough has been sufficiently kneaded when it is very smooth and gently pulls back into place when stretched.

3 Wrap the ball of dough tightly in clear food wrap and let rest for 1 hour, but 2 hours is even better if you have the time. If using within a few hours, leave it out on the kitchen counter, otherwise refrigerate it for up to 3 days. If you do refrigerate it, however, the dough may experience some discoloration (but it won't affect the flavor at all).

4 For instructions on rolling the dough, see the "Using a Pasta Maker" section on page 20.

5 Once fresh pasta has been cut, dust it with cocoa and then place it on a surface lightly dusted with cocoa and allow to dry for at least 15 minutes before cooking.

Chocolate Fettuccine with Pecan and Caramel Sauce

YIELD: 6 TO 8 SERVINGS • ACTIVE TIME: 15 MINUTES
TOTAL TIME: 20 MINUTES

While the combination of chocolate pasta and caramel does not exactly scream "traditional," it certainly makes for an occasional and unexpected treat. Both children and chocolate lovers will love it.

INGREDIENTS

4½ tablespoons unsalted butter

⅔ cup pecans, crushed

Salt, to taste

¾ cup light brown sugar, firmly packed

½ cup heavy cream

1 teaspoon vanilla extract

¾ pound Chocolate Pasta Dough (see pages 250–251), rolled out to 1/16-inch thick and cut into fettuccine

Chocolate shavings, for garnish

Raspberries, for garnish

1 Heat a small skillet for 2 to 3 minutes over low heat. Add 1 tablespoon of the butter and raise the heat to medium. Once it's melted, add the pecans and cook, while stirring continuously, until they give off toasty fragrance, about 2 minutes. Add 2 pinches of salt and stir. Transfer to a plate and let cool. Wipe out the skillet with a paper towel.

2 Put a large pot of water on to boil. While the water heats, put the skillet you toasted the pecans in over low heat. After 1 minute, add 3 tablespoons of the butter, the brown sugar, cream, and a pinch of salt and raise the heat to medium-low. Cook, while whisking gently, until the sauce thickens, 5 to 7 minutes. Stir in the vanilla and cook for another minute. Stir in the toasted pecans, remove the pan from heat, and cover.

3 When the pasta water is boiling, add salt (1 tablespoon for every 4 cups water) and stir. Add the pasta and cook until the pasta is tender but still very firm. Right before draining the pasta, reserve ¼ cup of the pasta

water. Return the empty pot to the stove. Immediately turn the heat to high and add the remaining butter and the reserved pasta water. Add the drained pasta and toss until the water is absorbed. Add the sauce and cook, mixing continuously, for 1 to 2 minutes. Ladle the pasta into warmed bowls and garnish with chocolate shavings and raspberries.

Chocolate Fettuccine with Pears, Candied Ginger, and Gorgonzola Cheese

Though this dessert calls for flambéing, a technique where food is spritzed with alcohol and briefly lit on fire, it is delicious with or without this additional step (if you opt to flambé, however, be sure use 80 proof alcohol; less is too weak, more is a fire hazard).

1 Place the pear slices on paper towels to drain. Heat a large skillet over medium heat for 2 to 3 minutes and then add the butter. Once it has melted, raise the heat to medium-high and add the pear slices. Let them cook undisturbed for 2 to 3 minutes. Gently turn them over and cook until the other side has browned, another 2 minutes.

2 Add the liquor to the pan and light with a long match, making sure to stand back from the stove when you do this. When the flames have subsided, swirl the skillet to move the pears around. Add the ginger and cook for 2 more minutes. Remove the pan from heat and cover.

3 Bring a large pot of water to a boil. When the pasta water is boiling, add salt (1 tablespoon for every 4 cups water) and stir. Add the pasta and cook until the pasta is soft but still very firm. Right before draining the pasta, reserve ¼ cup of the pasta water. Return the empty pot to the stove. Immediately turn the heat to high and add the remaining butter and the reserved pasta water. Add the drained pasta and Gorgonzola crumbles and cook, while tossing, until the crumbles begin to melt, about 2 minutes.

4 Divide the pasta between four warm bowls. Top with the pears and the sauce. Garnish with chocolate shavings and hazelnuts before serving.

INGREDIENTS

4 Anjou pears, cored and thinly sliced

4 tablespoons unsalted butter

2 tablespoons brandy or cognac

⅓ cup candied ginger, chopped

¾ pound Chocolate Pasta Dough (see pages 250–251), rolled out to ¹⁄₁₆-inch thick and cut into fettuccine

⅓ cup Gorgonzola cheese, crumbled

3 tablespoons chocolate shavings, for garnish

3 tablespoons hazelnuts, toasted and chopped, for garnish

INGREDIENTS

7 tablespoons unsalted butter, plus more for greasing the dish

Salt, to taste

½ pound angel hair pasta

1 teaspoon ground cinnamon

¾ cup slivered almonds

¾ cup raisins

¾ cup pistachios, shelled and chopped

½ cup caster sugar, plus 3½ tablespoons

¼ cup ice water

Whipped cream, for serving

Kataifi Pudding

Kataifi is a popular Greek dessert traditionally made with a pastry dough of the same name. This particular recipe bypasses the dough in favor of the far easier-to-find angel hair pasta.

1 Preheat the oven to 325°F and butter a 9 x 9-inch baking dish. Bring a large pot of water to a boil. When the pasta water is boiling, add salt (1 tablespoon for every 4 cups water) and stir. Add the pasta and cook 3 minutes less than the directed time. Reserve ¼ cup of the pasta water, drain the pasta, and set aside. Return the empty pot to the stove. Immediately turn the heat to high and add 4 tablespoons of the butter and the reserved pasta water. Add the drained pasta and cook. Add the cinnamon and toss for 1 to 2 minutes. Remove the pot from heat.

2 Transfer ⅓ of the cooked pasta to the prepared baking dish. Sprinkle half of the almonds, raisins, pistachios, and sugar over the top. Add another ⅓ of the cooked pasta and sprinkle with the remaining almonds, raisins, pistachios, and sugar.

Top with the remaining pasta. Cut the remaining butter into small pieces and dot the top with them. Place on the center rack of the oven, reduce the temperature to 300°F, and bake for 25 minutes.

3 While it bakes, put the remaining sugar in a small saucepan over low heat and stir until it melts and turns golden brown. Remove from the heat and very slowly and carefully (it will splatter a bit) add the water. Return the pan to the heat and stir until the mixture thickens, about 4 minutes.

4 After 25 minutes, remove the dish from the oven and pour the sauce evenly over the top. Return to the oven to bake until the topping is golden brown, about 5 minutes. Top with whipped cream and serve.

Angel Hair in Chocolate Sauce

**YIELD: 8 SERVINGS • ACTIVE TIME: 15 MINUTES
TOTAL TIME: 2½ TO 3½ HOURS**

One of Italy's few authentic pasta desserts, this sweet, chocolaty treat comes straight from Orvieto, a lovely city in the central Italian region of Umbria.

1 Combine the chocolate, sugar, and heavy cream in a small saucepan and cook over low heat. Stir until the chocolate melts and the mixture is smooth. Remove from heat and set aside.

2 Heat a small skillet over medium-low heat for 2 to 3 minutes. Add the butter, cook until it is melted, and then add the hazelnuts and raise the heat to medium. Stir continuously with a wooden spoon until they look slightly toasted and are giving off a wonderful fragrance. Add a pinch of salt, stir, remove from heat, and let cool.

3 Combine the hazelnuts, orange zest, honey, and allspice in another small saucepan, season with salt and cook over low heat, while stirring, until the honey has liquefied

and everything is well combined. Remove from the heat.

4 Bring a large pot of water to a boil. When the water is boiling, add salt (1 tablespoon for every 4 cups water) and stir. Add the pasta and cook for 2 minutes less than the directed time. Reserve ¼ cup of the pasta water, drain the pasta, and set aside. Return the empty pot to the stove. Immediately turn the heat to high and add the reserved pasta water. Add the drained pasta and toss. Add the chocolate sauce and cook, while tossing continuously, until the pasta is completely coated. Remove from heat.

5 Butter a 1-quart baking dish and then place half of the pasta in it. Pour the honey mixture over the pasta and then spread with

INGREDIENTS

3½ oz. 70 percent cocoa dark chocolate, chopped

3 tablespoons caster sugar

⅔ cup heavy cream

½ tablespoon butter, plus more for greasing the baking dish

1¼ cups hazelnuts, chopped

Salt, to taste

Zest of 1 orange

¼ cup honey

¼ teaspoon ground allspice

½ pound angel hair pasta

Whipped cream, for serving

a rubber spatula. Top with the rest of the angel hair. Cover and refrigerate for 2 to 3 hours to allow the noodles to set. Remove from the refrigerator at least 1 hour before serving. Cut into slices, top with a dollop of whipped cream, and serve.

Fried Angel Hair Nests with Honey, Dates, and Pistachios

**YIELD: 4 TO 6 SERVINGS • ACTIVE TIME: 30 MINUTES
TOTAL TIME: 45 MINUTES**

Delicate nests of angel hair provide a crunchy backdrop for moist and chewy dates, or any candied fruit you desire, in this dish.

1 Bring a large pot of water to a boil. When the water is boiling, season with salt and sugar (1 tablespoon for every 4 cups water) and stir. Add the pasta and cook for 2 minutes less than the directed time. Drain the pasta, rinse under cold water, and drain again. Transfer to a bowl, add the sesame oil, and toss to coat.

2 While the pasta cooks, place the honey in a microwave-safe bowl and microwave on high until it liquefies and becomes easy to pour, 20 to 30 seconds. Remove from the microwave and stir in the dates.

3 Pour enough vegetable oil in a large skillet to cover the bottom by ¼ inch. Turn the heat to medium-high. Once the surface of the oil begins to glisten, add the pasta to the skillet by twirling it around a fork to create small nests. Carefully place them in the hot oil and cook until golden and crisp at the edges, 30 to 60 seconds on each side. Transfer the crisp nests to a paper towel-lined plate to absorb excess oil. Repeat until all the pasta has been cooked.

4 Arrange the crisp pasta nests on serving plates. Drizzle with the honey-and-date mixture and garnish with pistachios and cinnamon.

INGREDIENTS

Salt, to taste

Sugar, to taste

½ pound angel hair pasta

1 tablespoon sesame oil

⅓ cup honey

3 tablespoons dates, minced

Vegetable oil, for frying

Pistachios, shelled and crushed, for garnish

Cinnamon, for garnish

INGREDIENTS

Rind from 1 lemon,
cut into strips

2 cups whole milk,
plus more as needed

2 teaspoons
vanilla extract

1 teaspoon dark rum

3 tablespoons
unsalted butter

1 cinnamon stick

½ cup sugar

4½ oz. vermicelli,
broken into
2-inch pieces

3 large egg yolks,
beaten

Ground cinnamon,
for dusting

Portuguese Vermicelli Pudding

YIELD: 4 SERVINGS • ACTIVE TIME: 10 MINUTES
TOTAL TIME: 30 MINUTES

A special place on Christmas dinner tables throughout Portugal is reserved for this treat. Much like rice pudding, this noodle pudding is sweet, soothingly soft, creamy, and loved by all.

1 Place the lemon rind, milk, vanilla, rum, butter, cinnamon stick, and sugar in a medium saucepan and cook, while stirring, over medium heat until the sugar dissolves. Slowly bring to a gentle boil, reduce the heat to low, cover, and simmer for 5 minutes.

2 Discard the lemon rind and cinnamon stick, raise the heat to medium-high, and bring to a boil.

3 Add the pasta and cook, while stirring occasionally, for 10 minutes (you want to slightly overcook the pasta in this recipe). When the pasta is very soft and most of the liquid has been absorbed, remove the pan from heat and let cool for 10 minutes.

4 Slowly add one spoonful of the warm pasta mixture to the beaten eggs and stir until well combined. Add another spoonful and mix until well combined. Add the tempered eggs to the pasta mixture and stir until well combined. If the mixture seems too thick, add more milk, 1 tablespoon at a time, until the thickness is similar to that of rice pudding. Transfer the pudding to four shallow serving bowls and top with cinnamon.

INGREDIENTS

4 tablespoons unsalted butter, melted, plus more for greasing the baking dish

½ cup Marsala wine

½ cup raisins

Salt, to taste

1 pound wide egg noodles

6 large eggs

8 oz. cream cheese, softened

1½ cups sour cream

1½ cups cottage cheese

1 cup sugar

10 large dried dates, pitted and minced

Lokshen Kugel

This versatile and filling egg noodle casserole is a traditional Ashkenazic dish that is often served on Shabbat and for Jewish holidays.

1 Preheat the oven to 375°F. Butter a 9 x 13-inch baking dish. Add the wine to a 4-cup Pyrex measuring cup and heat in the microwave for 30 seconds. Add the raisins and let them soak for 20 minutes. Drain the raisins and place them on a paper towel to absorb any excess liquid.

2 Bring a large pot of water to a boil. Once it's boiling, add salt (1 tablespoon for every 4 cups water) and stir. Add the noodles and cook for ¾ of the time directed on the package. Drain, rinse under cold water, and drain well again. Return the cooked noodles to the pot.

3 While the noodles are cooking, place the eggs, cream cheese, sour cream, cottage cheese, melted butter, sugar, and a pinch of salt in a food processor and puree until well combined and creamy.

Have the mixture ready to add to the just-drained noodles.

4 Immediately add the cheese mixture to the pot with the drained noodles and toss until well combined. Add the soaked raisins and the dates and toss again. Pour the noodle mixture into the prepared baking dish. If not ready to bake the kugel, cover and refrigerate for up to 48 hours (bring it back to room temperature before proceeding).

5 Place the dish on the center rack. Lower the oven temperature to 350°F. Bake until the middle of the kugel has set and the noodles sprouting out of the kugel have turned a caramel color, about 1 hour. Remove from the oven and let rest for 30 minutes before slicing. Serve warm or at room temperature.

Blueberry Varenyky

A staple in Eastern European countries for centuries, varenyky are sweet- or savory-filled noodles shaped like half-moons. This fruity version makes for a satisfying snack or dessert.

1 Prepare the filling. Place ⅔ of the blueberries in a medium saucepan. Add the sugar and lemon zest and stir. Turn the heat to medium and cook, while stirring occasionally, until the blueberries burst and release their juice, about 4 minutes. Reduce the heat to low and simmer, uncovered, for 18 to 20 minutes. The mixture should be very thick. Stir in the remaining blueberries, remove the pan from heat, and let cool completely.

2 Prepare the dough. Put the flour and salt in a large bowl. Add the 4 tablespoons of butter and sour cream and beat on medium speed with a standing mixer until the dough looks crumbly, about 5 minutes. Add the beaten egg to a measuring cup and add just enough water for the mixture to measure ¾ cup. Beat the egg and water until well blended and pour into the mixing bowl. Mix on medium speed until the dough holds together in a ball. If it's sticky, add in more flour, a teaspoon at a time, until the dough is smooth and not sticky.

3 Transfer the dough to a lightly floured work surface and, using a lightly floured rolling pin, roll it out to ⅛-inch thickness. Using a 3-inch stamp, biscuit, or cookie cutter, cut it into as many rounds as possible. Place the rounds on a lightly floured parchment paper-lined baking sheet so they don't touch. When you have as many as you can fit in a single layer, cover them with another piece of parchment, sprinkle with flour, and keep arranging the rounds in the same way.

4 Place a round in the palm of your slightly cupped hand and hold it so that it takes the shape of a taco. Place 1 teaspoon of filling in the center. Using your thumb and index finger, firmly pinch the edges together to form a tight seal. You'll want this seal, or seam, to be between $\frac{1}{4}$ and $\frac{1}{2}$ inch wide. Pat the sealed varenyky gently to evenly distribute the filling. Check for holes (patch them with a little bit of dough) and make sure the seal is tight. Reserve any leftover filling.

5 Bring a large pot of water to a boil. Once it's boiling, add salt (1 tablespoon for every 4 cups water) and the oil (to prevent any sticking) and stir. You will need to cook the varenyky in batches. Using a rounded slotted spoon, lower the varenyky into the boiling water. Stir for 1 minute to prevent them from sticking to the bottom. When the dumplings float to the surface, cook them for another 3 minutes. While the first batch of varenyky boils, melt the 5 tablespoons of butter in a microwave or over low heat. Remove the varenyky from the water using a large slotted spoon, and let them drain for a few seconds over the pot. Transfer to a warmed platter, top them with a tablespoon or so of melted butter, and gently toss. Tent loosely with aluminum foil to keep them warm while you cook the remaining varenyky. Dust the varenyky with confectioners' sugar and top with the leftover filling, if there is any.

INGREDIENTS

For the Filling

1 pound fresh blueberries, picked over for stems and rinsed

1 tablespoon sugar

Zest of 1 lemon

For the Dough

3 cups all-purpose flour, plus more as needed

½ teaspoon salt, plus more to taste

4 tablespoons unsalted butter, plus 5 tablespoons for drizzling

⅔ cup sour cream at room temperature

1 large egg, beaten

1 tablespoon vegetable oil

Confectioners' sugar, for dusting

Index

Recipes provided in the text are indicated in italics.

ABOUT CIDER MILL PRESS BOOK PUBLISHERS

Good ideas ripen with time. From seed to harvest, Cider Mill Press brings fine reading, information, and entertainment together between the covers of its creatively crafted books. Our Cider Mill bears fruit twice a year, publishing a new crop of titles each spring and fall.

"Where Good Books Are Ready for Press"

Visit us online at
cidermillpress.com
or write to us at
PO Box 454
12 Spring St.
Kennebunkport, Maine 04046